GLIMPSES OF GLORY

Glimpses of Glory

A selection of short studies
by

Dudley Fifield

THE CHRISTADELPHIAN
404 Shaftmoor Lane
Hall Green
Birmingham B28 8SZ

2012

First published 2012

ISBN 978-0-85189-199-6

Cover Artwork: Justin Allfree

*Printed and bound in Malta
by*
Gutenberg Press Ltd.

FOREWORD

DUDLEY FIFIELD (pictured) was an ardent Bible student and a prolific writer. His consideration of the Psalms, undertaken over many years and appearing in part in *The Bible Student*, resulted in the substantial three-volume work *The Praises of Israel* published by the CMPA, between 2008 and 2010. The third volume was completed while he was seriously ill and we are thankful that he was spared long enough to finish it. Although I never had the privilege of meeting Dudley, I feel I came to know him through editing the second volume in that series.

Glimpses of Glory is a collection of some of his many articles that appeared in *The Christadelphian* from 2003 to 2011, chosen to represent the wide range of subjects that he considered and expounded. It demonstrates his ability as a Bible student, underlying which was a deep affection for the things of God. It is inevitable in producing this book that the topics and aspects that I found particularly interesting and helpful should take precedence but, given their wide range within the scriptures, it is hoped that the result will provide something for everyone.

Throughout these short studies Dudley's sincere reverence for the word of God is evident and they demonstrate his comprehensive interest in all its aspects. While Dudley may have had a special love of the Psalms he did not restrict his studies to certain books but considered the whole counsel of God. The articles are presented here largely as they were originally published in the magazine.

It has been a great pleasure to read through the articles once more and it is hoped that this selection will be enjoyed by others who wish to have a miscellany of relatively short expositions that not only provide insights into the riches of God's word but also helpful exhortation. May the author's delight in God's law and the enthusiasm he had for its study prove infectious to today's readers, allowing them to glimpse something of the Father's glory.

JOHN M. HELLAWELL

CONTENTS

1

PAUL AND THE ECCLESIA AT THESSALONICA

ONE might get the impression from a cursory reading of Acts 17 (verses 1-10) that when Paul and Silas preached the Gospel in Thessalonica they spent only a limited time in that city:

"And Paul, as his manner was, went in unto them, and three sabbath days reasoned with them out of the scriptures, opening and alleging, that Christ must needs have suffered, and risen again from the dead; and that this Jesus, whom I preach unto you, is Christ. And some of them believed, and consorted with Paul and Silas; and of the devout Greeks a great multitude, and of the chief women not a few."

(verses 2-4)

On three consecutive sabbaths (two weeks) Paul preached in the synagogue, receiving a mixed reception from the Jews and a much more enthusiastic welcome from the devout Greeks who had associated themselves with the worship of Israel's God. The record in Acts then tells how the unbelieving Jews resorted to riotous behaviour:

"But the Jews which believed not, moved with envy, took unto them certain lewd fellows of the baser sort, and gathered a company, and set all the city on an uproar, and assaulted the house of Jason, and sought to bring them out to the people. And when they found them not, they drew Jason and certain brethren unto the rulers of the city, crying, These that have turned the world upside down are come hither also ... saying that there is another king, one Jesus. And they troubled the people and the rulers of the city ... And when they had taken security of Jason, and of the other, they let them go. And the brethren

1

immediately sent away Paul and Silas by night unto Berea." (verses 5-10)

It was necessary for Paul and Silas to remove in haste to Berea for their own safety .

The brevity of this account could lead to the conclusion that Paul and Silas spent only a few weeks in the city. However, when we read Paul's epistles to the believers at Thessalonica it becomes evident that between the preaching in the synagogue and the incitement to riot there was actually a more prolonged period during which Paul, barred from the synagogue, preached to the pagan population of the city: "(they) turned to God from idols to serve the living and true God" (1 Thessalonians 1:9).

It was not an easy period but was characterised by much opposition to the work, no doubt stirred up by the unbelieving Jews, for, says Paul, "we were bold in our God to speak unto you the gospel of God with much contention" (2:2). The Thessalonian believers were themselves subject to persecution from their own countrymen (2:14), and had "received the word in much affliction" (1:6).

Paul's example

During this period Paul and his companions behaved themselves in an exemplary manner:

"For ye remember, brethren, our labour and travail: for labouring night and day, because we would not be chargeable unto any of you, we preached unto you the gospel of God. Ye are witnesses, and God also, how holily and justly and unblameably we behaved ourselves among you that believe." (2:9,10)

The words "labour" and "travail" imply physical toil and manual labour, and the determination of Paul and his companions not to be a burden to these Gentile converts is emphasised by the words *night and day*. This, of course, was a characteristic of Paul's conduct in his preaching of the Gospel (see Acts 18:1-3; 20:33-35) and it is an indication that he was a true shepherd of the

2

flock. The behaviour of the apostles amongst them, together with the power of the message preached, made a tremendous impression upon those who embraced the hope of the Gospel:

"... ye know what manner of men we were among you for your sake. And ye became followers (RV, 'imitators') of us and of the Lord."

(1 Thessalonians 1:5,6)

The believer's response

The new found faith of the Thessalonian believers and their changed way of life was something they wanted to share with others:

"For from you sounded out the word of the Lord not only in Macedonia and Achaia, but also in every place your faith to God-ward is spread abroad." (1:8)

Their response to the Gospel was a matter of delight to Paul and while he was among them there was a wonderful sense of joy and fulfilment which they shared in each other's company:

"So being affectionately desirous of you, we were willing to have imparted unto you, not the gospel of God only, but also our own souls, because ye were dear unto us." (2:8)

"For what is our hope, or joy, or crown of rejoicing? Are not even ye in the presence of our Lord Jesus Christ at his coming? For ye are our glory and joy." (2:19,20)

Paul's anxiety

We cannot fail to detect the deep affection and friendship that existed between Paul and the Thessalonians. Driven by the hatred of the Jews, from Berea also, and compelled by circumstances to wait at Athens for Titus and Timothy, Paul's anxiety to hear of their welfare and his longing to see them again was intense:

"But we, brethren, being taken from you for a short time in presence, not in heart, endeavoured the more

3

abundantly to see your face with great desire. Wherefore we would have come unto you, even I Paul, once and again; but Satan hindered us." (2:17,18)

When eventually Paul was brought news by Timothy concerning their spiritual progress and well-being, he felt an overwhelming sense of relief and joy. He was comforted in his afflictions by the knowledge that their longing for him was as great as his for them (3:6-10).

There emerges from these considerations a remarkable picture of what the Truth can do for people. It is difficult for us to appreciate fully the kind of lives these new believers had lived in a pagan society where life revolved around a multiplicity of gods. Almost everything in daily life was in some way linked to idol worship, and unbridled lust and debauchery was never far away from their experience. In Paul and his companions they had seen demonstrated a way of life that gave a sense of joy and fulfilment; a peace of heart beyond their wildest expectations. It met their deepest needs; it released them from the bondage of sin; the vanity and emptiness of a life that left them with a sense of disgust and disillusionment.

We must never fail to preach the first principles of the Gospel message, for an understanding of the mind and purpose of God is absolutely vital to salvation. Nevertheless, perhaps we can learn from the example of the Thessalonians the value of emphasising the benefits of a consecrated life in the godless society in which we live. It may be that this is something we neglect to give the prominence it deserves in our preaching. Needless to say, if we preach it we should also live it, showing the change that the Lord Jesus has wrought in our lives too.

The life of Christ

The believers at Thessalonica had been attracted and won by the message preached and by the manner of life Paul and his companions lived amongst them. It would be a mistake, however, to believe that they were concerned with their own image. They were at pains to emphasise that they too had experienced the transforming power of the Gospel. They did not wish to project themselves, but the Lord Jesus Christ. Thus the Thessalonians became *"imitators of us and of the Lord"*.

A careful reading of both epistles reveals that the Lord Jesus was central to the message Paul and his companions preached. The accusation levelled against them when they were described as having turned the world upside down was that they did "contrary to the decrees of Caesar, saying that there is another king, one Jesus" (Acts 17:7).

Of course the Lord Jesus was always at the very heart of the Gospel message, but the person of the Lord and the life he lived appears to have been particularly dear to the Thessalonians and they longed for nothing more than to be with him. Notice that on fifteen occasions in these two epistles Paul refers to "our Lord Jesus Christ" (see 1 Thessalonians 1:3; 2:19; 3:11,13 etc.). The words are, of course, not unique to these epistles, but nowhere (except 2 Peter – seven occasions) is there such a remarkable emphasis upon the intimacy of the relationship they enjoyed with the Lord Jesus. It was an experience the Thessalonians shared with Paul, Silas and Timothy, for he is *"our* Lord Jesus". It was this association with him that had bound them all together in the life they lived. There were many gods and lords, but only one Lord Jesus Christ. He was *their* Lord, they belonged to him and he to them, and in this association they rejoiced. They longed for nothing more than to be with him, to be in his presence, to share with him in person, in glorious incorruptible bodies, the life they had come to know through the apostles.

To be in his presence

Thus the apostle emphasises that it is "the Lord *himself* (who) shall descend from heaven" (4:16). It is "our Lord Jesus *himself*, and God, even our Father, which hath loved us, and hath given us everlasting consolation and good hope through grace ..." (2 Thessalonians 2:16).

What then was their hope? How did Paul express it? It was to be with the Lord Jesus, to be in his presence in the day of his coming, numbered amongst the company of the saints:

"For what is our hope, or joy, or crown of rejoicing? Are not even ye in the presence of our Lord Jesus Christ at his coming?" (1 Thessalonians 2:19)

"To the end he may stablish your hearts unblameable in holiness before God, even our Father, at the coming of our Lord Jesus Christ with all his saints." (3:13)

"Then we which are alive and remain shall be caught up together with them in the clouds, to meet the Lord in the air: and so shall we ever be with the Lord. Wherefore comfort one another with these words." (4:17,18)

"For God hath not appointed us to wrath, but to obtain salvation by our Lord Jesus Christ, who died for us, that, whether we wake or sleep, we should live together with him." (5:9,10)

"Now we beseech you, brethren, by the coming of our Lord Jesus Christ, and by our gathering together unto him ..." (2 Thessalonians 2:1)

The exhortation for us

The example of our brethren and sisters at Thessalonica poses some very searching questions for us. How do we feel about the life to which we have been called? Is it our overwhelming desire to be numbered amongst the saints of all ages, to be in the presence of the Lord Jesus when he comes in his glory? Are we comforted by this thought in the midst of all life's troubles and adversities? Do we appreciate the vanity and emptiness of all that the world has to offer, so that more and more we grow in our appreciation of the true value of the life to which we have been called in Christ?

The promise is:

"And to you who are troubled rest with us, when the Lord Jesus shall be revealed from heaven with his mighty angels, in flaming fire taking vengeance on them that know not God, and that obey not the gospel of our Lord Jesus Christ: who shall be punished with everlasting destruction from the presence of the Lord, and from the glory of his power; when he shall come to be glorified in his saints, and to be admired in all them that believe (because our testimony among you was believed) in that day."

(1:7-10)

He will be glorified in the saints, for they have been delivered from sin and death by this work of salvation and his life is seen in them, for he is admired in all that believe. They have in every sense been conformed to his image and they shall "ever be with the Lord". If this is truly our desire, let us "comfort one another with these words".

2

"YOUR ADVERSARY THE DEVIL"

A CURSORY examination of the words of the Apostle Peter in his first epistle (chapter 5) should be enough to convince any unbiased reader that the danger presented by the devil to the believers to whom Peter wrote was not that of enticement or allurement to sin, but rather had to do with suffering and persecution:

"Be sober, be vigilant; because your adversary the devil, as a roaring lion, walketh about, seeking whom he may devour: whom resist stedfast in the faith, knowing that the same afflictions are accomplished in your brethren that are in the world. But the God of all grace, who hath called us unto his eternal glory by Christ Jesus, after that ye have suffered a while, make you perfect, stablish, strengthen, settle you. To him be glory and dominion for ever and ever. Amen."

(1 Peter 5:8-11)

The devil was seeking whom he might devour and the same afflictions (RV, sufferings) that they experienced were also being accomplished in their brethren throughout the world. The assurance they had was that after they had suffered a while they should know the eternal glory to which God had called them. The devil is likened to a roaring lion and our understanding of the passage is enlarged if we appreciate that behind it there lies a fund of Old Testament allusions.

The Psalms

In the Psalms, lions are sometimes used to represent those evil men who sought to persecute and destroy God's servants and we want to look particularly at Psalm 22 a little later in this study. Some examples are:

"O LORD my God, in thee do I put my trust: save me from all them that persecute me, and deliver me: lest he tear my soul like a lion, rending it in pieces, while there is none to deliver." (Psalm 7:1,2)

"They have now compassed us in our steps: they have set their eyes bowing down to the earth; like as a lion that is greedy of his prey, and as it were a young lion lurking in secret places." (17:11,12)

See also Psalms 10:9,10; 35:16,17.

In addition, there are other passages where, although the lion is not mentioned, the figure of swallowing up, devouring or eating is used:

"Be merciful unto me, O God: for man would swallow me up; he fighting daily oppresseth me. Mine enemies would daily swallow me up: for they be many that fight against me, O thou most High." (Psalm 56:1,2)

"If it had not been the LORD who was on our side, when men rose up against us: then they had swallowed us up quick, when their wrath was kindled against us." (124:2,3)

See also Psalms 27:2; 35:25.

In all these passages the reference is, quite clearly, to the Psalmist's adversaries: those men who hated him and persecuted him; who if the opportunity presented itself would have swallowed him up (i.e., killed him).

Daniel and Paul

It is appropriate in this context that we consider briefly the experience of Daniel when faced by the jealousy of the "presidents and princes" of Babylon. Because he was "preferred above" them (literally, distinguished himself) they conspired to have him thrown into the den of lions. It does not seem inappropriate to think of the lions as representative of the presidents and princes who sought Daniel's life, and he was not swallowed up by them because God sent His angel and shut the lions' mouths.

9

The Apostle Paul seems to have had this incident in mind when he wrote to Timothy shortly before his death:

> "At my first answer no man stood with me, but all men forsook me: I pray God that it may not be laid to their charge. Notwithstanding the Lord stood with me, and strengthened me; that by me the preaching might be fully known, and that all the Gentiles might hear: and I was delivered out of the mouth of the lion. And the Lord shall deliver me from every evil work, and will preserve me unto his heavenly kingdom."
>
> (2 Timothy 4:16-18)

Paul was not thinking of a literal lion; he was not referring to the gladiators' arena, but with a wealth of Old Testament scripture to call on he was reflecting on his deliverance from the power of Rome at his first appearance before Nero's court. The Lord had stood with him as the angel had stood with Daniel and shut the lions' mouths.

Psalm 22

Returning to Peter's words in his first epistle, it would appear that he was making a direct reference to David's prophetic insight into the sufferings of the Lord Jesus Christ in Psalm 22:

> "I am a worm, and no man; a reproach of men, and despised of the people. All they that see me laugh me to scorn: they shoot out the lip, they shake the head ..." (verses 6,7)

> "Be not far from me; for trouble is near; for there is none to help. Many bulls have compassed me: strong bulls of Bashan have beset me round. They gaped upon me with their mouths, as a ravening and a roaring lion." (verses 11-13)

> "For dogs have compassed me: the assembly of the wicked have inclosed me: they pierced my hands and my feet. (verse 16)

David enters into the spirit of the Lord Jesus when he concludes this section of the Psalm with the words:

"Save me from the lion's mouth: for thou hast heard me from the horns of the unicorns." (verse 21)

The Lord's enemies, those who sought his life because of the challenge he presented, were like a roaring lion seeking to swallow him up. Now it is not difficult to identify just who was responsible for persecuting and crucifying the Lord Jesus. It was the powers of this world:

"For of a truth against thy holy child Jesus, whom thou hast anointed, both Herod, and Pontius Pilate, with the Gentiles, and the people of Israel, were gathered together, for to do whatsoever thy hand and thy counsel determined before to be done."

(Acts 4:27,28)

They were confederate together; an amalgam of the power of sin manifested in "the rulers of the darkness of this world" (Ephesians 6:12). They crucified the Lord Jesus to fulfil their own evil intentions, yet unwittingly they fulfilled the will and purpose of God. They constituted the devil, which, in the passages that have been considered, is a dramatic representation of sin in its external conflict with the Lord Jesus.

Conclusion

It was this same power that now threatened the believers to whom Peter addressed his letter. In an endeavour to compel them to deny the faith, it persecuted them and delivered them to death. As a roaring lion it would swallow them up.

It was Imperial Rome, eagerly prompted by the Jews and other groups who thought that their interests were threatened. This was the devil in its corporate form. In this mantle the threat is always from without; it is never the power of sin that operates within. Peter's exhortation was:

"Be sober, be vigilant … whom resist stedfast in the faith."

This is not a supernatural tempter therefore but a very real threat nonetheless – human nature manifested in its most awful and frightening ways.

3

WHAT DOES CHRIST MEAN TO US?

THE purpose of this study is to examine what the Lord Jesus Christ meant to the Apostle Paul. From this consideration we can then assess our own attitude towards the Lord Jesus and what he should mean to us.

Paul's constraint

Writing to the ecclesia at Corinth the apostle said:

"For the love of Christ constraineth us; because we thus judge, that if one died for all, then were all dead." (2 Corinthians 5:14)

The word translated "constraineth" conveys the idea of pressure or compulsion; in certain contexts it suggests preoccupation, as though nothing else mattered. So Paul's thinking was dominated by the love of Christ. He was preoccupied by it and would let nothing intrude into his life that might detract from it. He was a driven man who enjoyed a relationship with the Lord Jesus that ensured that he lived not for himself but for the one who loved him and died for him.

It was because of this that Paul was able to face such dreadful privations and cope with those intense personal sufferings that he catalogues in the second epistle to the Corinthians:

"Of the Jews five times received I forty stripes save one. Thrice was I beaten with rods, once was I stoned, thrice I suffered shipwreck, a night and a day I have been in the deep; in journeyings often, in perils of waters, in perils of robbers, in perils by mine own countrymen, in perils by the heathen, in perils in the city, in perils in the wilderness, in perils in the sea, in perils among false brethren; in weariness and painfulness, in watchings often, in hunger and thirst, in fastings often, in cold and nakedness." (11:24-27) We can but stand in awe, filled with wonder and amazement at the fortitude and resilience of this man who endured such a burden of adversity.

His changed ambitions

Paul had died with Christ and nothing could compare with the surpassing riches that he had found in him. He might have been a star shining in the Jewish heavens. He had the most impressive credentials; an impeccable pedigree. He had been a trained Pharisee, numbered amongst the spiritual elite in Israel. His way of life in Judaism was beyond reproach; he could not be faulted. Almost certainly he was a member of the Sanhedrin. He was a prince in Israel and the Jewish world lay at his feet. Before him there was a glittering future (Philippians 3:4-6), but he had died with Christ and those things that were gain to him he counted loss for Christ (verse 7). Everything that he looked for in life had changed:

> "How changed are my ambitions! Now I long to know Christ and the power shown by his resurrection." (verse 10, J. B. Phillips)

To know Christ had become Paul's preoccupation. Nothing else mattered. It was not just a matter of knowing *about* him, for intellectual knowledge was but the beginning of a process. What Paul longed for was an experiential knowledge that would involve a participation in the life that the Lord Jesus had lived – to know in his own experience the moral qualities that his Lord had exhibited.

Our aim in life

What then does Christ mean to us? How do we feel about the life he lived? Are we attracted by the beauty of his holiness, by the wonder of his moral excellence? This is the life to which he has called us, the life that will be lived in the kingdom.

Paul's ambition to know Christ was to be finally consummated in the resurrection from the dead (Philippians 3:11). He was not thinking simply of the emergence from the grave, for he knew that he would appear before the Judgement Seat of Christ. He was thinking of the whole process of resurrection that would see him transformed into Christ's image. He longed for nothing more than that he should share the life of the Lord Jesus in a glorified and incorruptible body.

Is that our aim in life? Do we, like the apostle, count all things but loss that we might win Christ? For Christ is the path and Christ the prize.

4

SIMON OF CYRENE

ONE of the thrilling things about Bible study is the manner in which we are sometimes led into the byways of knowledge by the record of seemingly unimportant information. A name, for example, that occurs in a certain context and then recurs in a different context. Again, there are clues to possible connections that at first might appear to be very tenuous. Yet when all the various pieces of information have been gathered together, a picture emerges and a conviction grows that we have discovered another insight into the work of God with an individual He has called to His kingdom.

We have such an example in the various references that follow. They all revolve around Simon of Cyrene and they can be discovered by a perusal of the many aids to Bible study available to us today.

Carrying the cross

God always has the right man in the right place at the right time. Such a man was Simon of Cyrene, who came from a Roman province in North Africa where there was a flourishing Jewish community. Whether he was a Jew of the dispersion or a proselyte we cannot be certain.

No doubt Simon had travelled to Jerusalem to keep the feast of Passover and when he set off that morning he could not have imagined the manner in which his life was to be changed for ever by the events of that day. What circumstances brought him to that particular place at that moment of time? What was there about this man that caused Roman soldiers to lay hold on him and compel him to carry the Lord's cross? That the Lord had need of him is beyond question and the service he performed was one that might equally have been undertaken by any number of individuals who lined the route to Golgotha.

But for Simon of Cyrene it was not just the hand of a Roman soldier that was laid upon him but it was also the hand of God. He was chosen to follow the Lord and to carry his cross. It was an unpleasant and distasteful task and whether he stayed to watch the crucifixion we cannot say with certainty. Given the circumstances we feel that he must have. However, such was the impression these experiences made upon him that ever afterwards he walked in the footsteps of the Master, bearing now his own cross.

How, it might be asked, can we know this to be true? The answer is that Mark's Gospel record gives us a little more information about this man:

"And they compel one Simon a Cyrenian, who passed by, coming out of the country, the father of Alexander and Rufus, to bear his cross." (Mark 15:21)

Clearly Alexander and Rufus were well known to those who first read Mark's Gospel record and the conclusion is inescapable that both they and Simon their father were numbered amongst those who believed in the Lord Jesus Christ.

Stephen's defence

Amongst those who disputed with Stephen were they of the synagogue of the Libertines and of the Cyrenians (Acts 6:9, see RV), and we might well wonder whether Simon and his family had been connected with this group in the past. If they had been they may well have sought to support Stephen in his defence of the Gospel, and when after Stephen's death a great persecution arose (Acts 8:1-4) they may well have become the particular target of those with whom they had previously been associated. This thought, of course, could be dismissed as pure conjecture but concerning those who were scattered abroad at this time we have some further information given in Acts 11:

"Now they which were scattered abroad upon the persecution that arose about Stephen travelled as far as Phenice, and Cyprus, and Antioch, preaching the word to none but unto the Jews only. And some of them were men of Cyprus and Cyrene, which, when they were come to Antioch, spake unto the Grecians, preaching the Lord Jesus. And the hand of the Lord was with them: and a great number believed, and turned unto the Lord."   (verses 19-21)

These men of Cyprus and Cyrene are not named but surely their names are written in heaven. Here were men of great spiritual insight for they are the first of whom it is recorded that they preached the Gospel to the Gentiles acting purely on their own initiative. They had almost certainly been influenced by the teaching of Stephen, for the burden of his message was that the God of Israel could not be confined by the walls of a building (i.e., the temple), nor by the boundaries of the land, for He was the God of all the earth. That Simon and his family were connected to Stephen is perhaps now seen to be possible even though still a little tenuous. In any event the direct result of their preaching was that Barnabas was sent from Jerusalem to investigate these events at Antioch and he hastened to Tarsus to bring Paul into the picture.

At Antioch

It was these events that set the scene for the launching of the first missionary journey, for –

"there were in the church that was at Antioch certain prophets and teachers; as Barnabas, and Simeon that was called Niger, and Lucius of Cyrene, and Manaen, which had been brought up with Herod the tetrarch, and Saul."   (Acts 13:1)

Interestingly, here was Lucius of Cyrene and we wonder whether he was one of those who first preached to the Gentiles. But also there was Simeon that was called Niger. The word Niger is of Latin origin and literally means 'black'. It was associated with Africa and the phrase has been variously translated as "Simeon the dark one" and "Simeon the African". As previously stated, Cyrene was in North Africa and this opens up the intriguing possibility that the individual referred to was in fact the Simon who carried the Lord's cross. He may well have been of mixed blood with a swarthy complexion, or indeed the reference might just have been to the place of his origin. It is well known that it was common amongst the Jews to use nicknames in this way. How wonderful to think that the man grasped by rough Roman hands to carry the Lord's cross was now numbered amongst that select band of individuals who under the direction of the Holy Spirit were responsible for sending the message of the cross into all the world.

Rufus chosen in the Lord

There is a further strand of evidence to be considered. We know from Mark's Gospel record that the name of one of Simon's sons was Rufus. In his epistle to the Romans Paul writes:

> "Salute Rufus chosen in the Lord, and his mother and mine."   (Romans 16:13)

How else could the apostle think of this man whose father had been compelled by Roman soldiers to carry the cross but was in very truth chosen of God to perform this task, and who thereafter, with all his family, followed in the footsteps of the man from Nazareth? And how was it that the apostle could come to speak of the wife of Simon and mother of Rufus as being a mother to him? Surely the evidence points to the time when Paul came to Antioch, when perhaps he had lodged in the home of Simon and enjoyed the hospitality of his wife who had been as a mother to him.

Conclusion

So the threads come together in an intriguing way, and present us with a wonderful picture of the hand of God at work in the life of an individual who ventured forth one day unaware of the momentous change that was to take place in his life. This was the first of a chain of circumstances that were finally to bring him to Antioch where he would be involved in one of the most important decisions in the history of the first century ecclesia – the launching of the message of the Gospel into the wider Roman world.

It is that same God who is active today to accomplish His purposes in our lives, and in the work of the ecclesias and those organisations responsible for the preaching of His word throughout the world. The methods He uses might be less spectacular and the ends achieved not as impressive, but they are nonetheless assurances to us that our Heavenly Father is still working with us "to take out of (the Gentiles) a people for his name" (Acts 15:14).

5

THE UNFORGIVING CREDITOR

WHEN Peter asked the Lord Jesus, "How oft shall my brother sin against me, and I forgive him? Till seven times?", he probably thought that he was making an extremely generous gesture. The Lord's response, "I say not unto thee, Until seven times: but, Until seventy times seven" (Matthew 18:21,22) must at first have left Peter with a sense of bewilderment. After all, humanly speaking, there are limits. A man would not be expected to suffer insult time and time again and continually offer forgiveness to the wrongdoer. But, of course, God turns human values upside down.

It has been suggested that the Lord Jesus was alluding to the words of Lamech in his notorious sword song:

"If Cain shall be avenged sevenfold, truly Lamech seventy and sevenfold."   (Genesis 4:24)

If this is indeed the case then the Lord Jesus is contrasting the natural man's desire for revenge to the uttermost with the spiritual man's willingness to forgive freely and without limit.

The King's compassion

To illustrate the point the Lord told the parable of the unforgiving creditor (Matthew 18:23-35). A certain king takes account of his servants and one is found who owed him ten thousand talents. The AV margin tells us that a talent was worth £240. On this basis the man owed a total of £2,400,000. This was an enormous amount, but if we allow for inflation, and try to express it in present day terms it would probably have risen to many billions of pounds. The point is that it was completely beyond the servant's ability to repay the debt he had incurred. In human terms it was an impossibility. There was no release; it was a burden he would have to carry throughout his life. He had no alternative but to cast himself on the mercy of his master:

> "The servant therefore fell down, and worshipped him, saying, Lord, have patience with me, and I will pay thee all." (18:26)

The king, beholding the utter ruin the servant had brought upon himself, had compassion on him and loosing him from his bond forgave him all. One can only imagine the sense of release a man in this position would have felt; the joy and gladness that would have filled his heart as a result of the love and compassion shown to him by his lord.

Our sinfulness

This section of the parable speaks to us in unmistakable terms of the wonder of God's forgiveness. Before Him we have incurred a debt, through sin, that it is utterly impossible for us to repay. Yet we rejoice in the knowledge that –

> "If we confess our sins, he is faithful and just to forgive us our sins, and to cleanse us from all unrighteousness." (1 John 1:9)

Through our Lord Jesus Christ God has lifted the burden and released us from the debt. The enormous sum that the man owed in the parable should bring home to us what a tremendous thing it is that God has done for us. Only an appreciation of our sinfulness and the gulf that it created between us and God, can ever truly convince us of the hopelessness of our plight. It is this experience that should fill us also with a sense of awe at the amazing thing that God has done in putting away our sins and continuing to offer us forgiveness if we seek it in the appointed way.

The example of David

This was something that David experienced in the matter of Bathsheba and Uriah the Hittite. When afterwards he meditated upon the grace and mercy of God, he wrote in Psalm 32:

"I acknowledged my sin unto thee, and mine iniquity have I not hid. I said, I will confess my transgressions unto the LORD; and thou forgavest the iniquity of my sin." (verse 5)

For David the result of his confession was that God forgave his sin. In the Hebrew text there is a great emphasis on the word "thou" that cannot be conveyed in the English translation. To demonstrate the emphasis some have suggested that the word should be repeated: "Thou, thou forgavest", thus indicating the sense of wonder and awe David felt at the realisation that God should have forgiven his sin that had been so great. This sense of wonder is something that should be part of the common experience of us all when we contemplate everything that God has done for us in the Lord Jesus Christ.

The "wicked servant"

The reaction of the man in the parable towards his fellow servant is an indication of how lamentably he had failed to appreciate the compassion of the king:

"The same servant went out, and found one of his fellowservants, which owed him an hundred pence: and he laid hands on him, and took him by the throat, saying, Pay me that thou owest. And his fellowservant fell down at his feet, and besought him, saying, Have patience with me, and I will pay thee all. And he would not: but went and cast him into prison, till he should pay the debt."

(Matthew 18:28-30)

He was owed one hundred pence. Interestingly, this was not an insignificant sum. In the parable of the labourers in the vineyard the agreed rate for a day's work was a penny (Matthew 20:2). One hundred pence would, therefore, be approximately three months' wages for a labourer. If, once again, we were to convert this into present day values then it would be approximately £4,000. In human terms this would be a debt not easily overlooked. The point that is being emphasised is that sometimes the wrong done by one man to another can be of a very grievous nature, and our natural instincts would not prompt us to forgive easily. The debt only fades into complete and utter insignificance when it is compared with the enormous, incalculable debt that the king had forgiven.

If we have appreciated the truly astonishing love of God towards us, and come to an understanding of the marvel of His forgiveness, then we too must recognise that the wrongs men do to us are of no real consequence compared with the debt of gratitude that we have incurred before God. Truly we have been taught of God to love one another (1 Thessalonians 4:9).

From the heart

In the parable the unforgiving creditor cast his fellow servant into prison. This can have a direct counterpart in our relationship with our brethren and sisters. We do not literally send them to prison but because of some wrong, real or imagined, we exclude them from our company. We ostracise them, ignore them, and count them unworthy of our fellowship. If we cannot find it in our hearts to forgive our brethren and sisters then neither will our Heavenly Father forgive us (Matthew 18:35).

It must be from our hearts, for it is possible to adopt an attitude of indifference towards those we feel have done us some wrong. We would do them no harm; we would not deliberately set out to hurt them; but our attitude towards them is completely negative, and because of this we do not take positive action to do them good.

The debt transferred

There is a final lesson that emerges from the parable that illustrates the point. There is a sense in which, having forgiven us the debt that we have incurred, God has as it were transferred it. The Apostle Paul writes in his epistle to the Romans:

> "I am debtor both to the Greeks, and to the Barbarians; both to the wise, and to the unwise."
>
> (Romans 1:14)

Again:

> "Owe no man anything, but to love one another."
>
> (13:8)

We show our appreciation of all that God has done for us by our attitude towards our fellow men. We seek to repay the debt that He has forgiven us by the love and concern that we show to others. We do it by the manner in which we seek to spread abroad the Gospel message that others might share with us the wonder of God's grace. A responsibility has been laid upon us and we too are debtors to our fellow men. We demonstrate the love and forgiveness that we have experienced by showing a like love to our brethren and sisters and indeed to all men.

In these ways we seek to repay, totally inadequately, the debt that we have incurred before God and which He in His mercy and compassion has forgiven us freely.

6

THE EVIL EYE

O talk of an evil eye with a superstitious man of the world would probably conjure up in his mind thoughts of sorcery and magic – a belief that a malicious look from an individual possessed by evil could somehow do harm to the person at whom it was directed.

The truth of the matter is quite different, for "an evil eye" is a Biblical expression that when examined in the contexts in which it occurs presents us with a very powerful word of exhortation.

The year of release

We find it, for example, in the book of Deuteronomy (chapter 15) where Moses instructs the people of Israel regarding the manner in which they were to show compassion towards one of their poor brethren. They were not to harden their hearts to his plight but they were to open their hands wide and lend him sufficient for his need (verses 7,8). In this context Moses continues:

"Beware that there be not a thought in thy wicked heart, saying, The seventh year, the year of release, is at hand; and thine eye be evil against thy poor brother, and thou givest him nought; and he cry unto the LORD against thee, and it be sin unto thee. Thou shalt surely give him, and thine heart shall not be grieved when thou givest unto him: because that for this thing the LORD thy God shall bless thee in all thy works, and in all that thou puttest thine hand unto."

(verses 9,10)

In the year of release all debts were cancelled. There was, therefore, a very real possibility that money lent shortly before the coming of that year would never be repaid. In these circumstances a covetous man could allow his heart to be hardened to his brother's need – blinded to the need for generosity of spirit to be shown by his love of money. In scriptural terms, to behave in this way was to have an evil eye.

The book of Proverbs contains similar counsel to the book of Deuteronomy:

"He that hath a bountiful eye (RV margin, 'good eye') shall be blessed; for he giveth of his bread to the poor." (22:9)

"He that hasteth to be rich hath an evil eye, and considereth not that poverty shall come upon him." (28:22)

"Labour not to be rich: cease from thine own wisdom. Wilt thou set thine eyes upon that which is not? For riches certainly make themselves wings; they fly away as an eagle toward heaven. Eat thou not the bread of him that hath an evil eye, neither desire thou his dainty meats. For as he thinketh in his heart, so is he. Eat and drink, saith he to thee; but his heart is not with thee." (23:4-7)

Clearly the opposite of an evil eye is a bountiful or good eye. The covetous man has little thought for the future beyond his desire to accumulate riches. They captivate his spirit and fill his heart so that he is blind to the spiritual poverty that will inevitably overtake him.

But riches can prove to be elusive and sometimes like a bird they will fly away and evade the grasp. In these circumstances a man might resort to dubious tactics to achieve his objectives. He might seek to cultivate the company of worldly-minded men who are rich and powerful, thinking that they might help him to gain the riches and power that have escaped his clutch. Beware says the proverb, for his hospitality and generosity will be a mask to hide his true motives. He will have achieved his position in life because he too has an evil eye. In his heart he will be seeking his own good and pursuing his own covetous desires. His apparent generosity will hide the niggardly spirit that really motivates him and his words will cover the fact that he is calculating the cost and begrudging every morsel that is eaten.

The evil eye, then, refers to that mean and niggardly spirit that out of a hard heart shows no consideration for the needs of the poor. It describes the covetous man who values riches and the power they bring above all else.

The single eye

The Old Testament connections that we have considered are carried over into the pages of the New Testament, where we find them upon the lips of the Lord Jesus. He said:

> "The light of the body is the eye: therefore when thine eye is single, thy whole body also is full of light; but when thine eye is evil, thy body also is full of darkness. Take heed therefore that the light which is in thee be not darkness. If thy whole body therefore be full of light, having no part dark, the whole shall be full of light, as when the bright shining of a candle doth give thee light." (Luke 11:34-36)

The light of the body is the eye. The eye does not disseminate light but receives it. Through it the body is, as it were, enlightened. If the eye is diseased all kinds of malfunctions can occur. Sight might be blurred; we could have double vision or even lose the ability to see altogether. So if the eye is single, as opposed to evil, the whole body will be full of light. As with the natural so also with the spiritual. The eye becomes a perfect figure to represent our ability to understand. Even in everyday speech when a thing is perceived we say, "I see". Thus the Apostle Paul could pray for the Ephesians –

> "that the God of our Lord Jesus Christ, the Father of glory, may give unto you the spirit of wisdom and revelation in the knowledge of him: the eyes of your understanding being enlightened; that ye may know

what is the hope of his calling, and what the riches of the glory of his inheritance in the saints." (1:17,18)

Of the Greek word translated "single", Strong's Concordance tells us that figuratively it means 'clear'. How therefore can we ensure that our spiritual sight is healthy, able to discern unhindered by any distraction the things that God would have us to understand? The Psalmist says:

"The entrance of thy words giveth light; it giveth understanding unto the simple." (119:130)

It is achieved through our reading and meditation upon the word of God. Its sweet influence will ensure that we develop that bountiful and generous spirit that allows no place for covetousness because we have come to appreciate the wonder of the things that God has done for us in the Lord Jesus Christ.

Of course, it is not just covetousness that can blind us. Paul exhorted the Colossians:

"Servants obey in all things your masters according to the flesh; not with eyeservice, as menpleasers; but in singleness of heart, fearing God." (3:22)

All manner of things can warp our outlook. The perverseness of human nature is such that anything we set our hearts on can cause our perception of truth to be distorted. Stubbornness, bitterness of heart, refusal to forgive, pride in our own achievements – in fact all the works of the flesh – can blind us to the reality of a situation. How needful is the exhortation to take heed therefore that "the light that is in thee" be not darkness (Matthew 6:23). If the eye of our understanding malfunctions, if our eye is not single but evil, then the light of God's word will not shine into our hearts and the light that is in us will in fact be darkness.

The conscience

In practical terms how do we develop a good conscience? How do we develop, not a clear conscience, but one that functions properly, that has been trained to discern between right and wrong? It is this ability to be conscious of ourselves, to stand as it were outside and to look into our hearts, that distinguishes us from the animals. The book of Proverbs describes this quality:

> "The spirit of man is the candle of the LORD, searching all the inward parts of the belly."   (20:27)

If we have allowed the word of God to have its proper effect upon us; if through constant reading and meditation the eye of our understanding has been enlightened to discern between right and wrong, then our whole body will be full of light.

A final example

We are carried back to our opening consideration of Deuteronomy 15 by the words of the Apostle Paul when he spoke of the generosity of the Macedonian ecclesias in contributing to the collection for the saints at Jerusalem:

> "Moreover, brethren, we do you to wit of the grace of God bestowed on the churches of Macedonia; how that in a great trial of affliction the abundance of their joy and their deep poverty abounded unto the riches of their liberality."   (2 Corinthians 8:1,2)

The RV margin reads for "liberality": "Greek, singleness"; and the word is indeed the very same as that which the Lord Jesus contrasted with an evil eye in Luke 11. In other words, their generosity of spirit was such that their only concern was for the need of their brethren and sisters at Jerusalem. They were not blinded by considerations of their own welfare, but with a singleness of purpose they gladly gave as they were able.

Exhorting the Corinthians to follow the example of their Macedonian brethren, Paul uses language that appears to be based on the words of Moses – "thine heart shall not be grieved when thou givest unto him" (Deuteronomy 15:10):

"Every man according as he purposeth in his heart, so let him give; not grudgingly, or of necessity: for God loveth a cheerful giver." (2 Corinthians 9:7)

Interestingly, the word rendered "singleness" recurs in this chapter – on this occasion translated "bountifulness":

"Being enriched in every thing to all bountifulness (AV margin, 'liberality'; RV margin, 'singleness'), which causeth through us thanksgiving to God."

(verse 11)

Experiencing and appreciating the goodness of God towards them, Paul's desire is that their liberality might abound.

Our response

What then is the message for us? We live in a society that is absorbed with material things. Money has become one of the ways in which a man's worth is measured. Covetousness has become one of the besetting sins of our age. A nice house, beautifully furnished, situated in a desirable location; a top of the range car, a boat perhaps, or a holiday home – all these things the worldly man covets and works to achieve, with perhaps a bit stored away for 'a rainy day'. This, of course, should not be our motivation in life, for the word of God teaches us different values. If that word has had its proper effect upon "the eye of our understanding", then our whole body will be full of light. There will be no malfunction to produce a distorted outlook, but we shall see clearly the things that really matter. The danger, however, is very real, for the gods of this world can appear extremely attractive and covetousness can creep into our hearts in a most insidious way. The work of the Truth demands not just physical effort but also our financial support. Is our eye single or evil? Do we first ensure that all our own needs, real or imagined, have been taken care of before we consider what contributions we can make from that which remains?

Do we give grudgingly or bountifully and cheerfully? We have the ability with the word of God as our guide

31

to search the innermost parts of our being. If we cannot see that the things of God's Truth must come first, if our overwhelming desire is to obtain those things the world has to offer, then truly the light that is in us is darkness.

As we examine ourselves how much we need to take heed to the words of the Apostle Paul:

"He that giveth, let him do it with simplicity (RV margin, 'singleness')."   (Romans 12:8)

7

"WHAT SEEKEST THOU?"

SOMETIMES the scriptural record of events leaves us with questions that we can only speculate about in seeking answers. Such is the case in the account of Joseph's dreams and the reaction of his brothers. After he had related their content, both his father and his brethren remonstrated with him because of the clear implications they contained.

While his brethren burned with envy and jealousy, however, his father observed the saying and no doubt pondered its significance in his heart. We can imagine the strained atmosphere that must have existed within the family and this must surely have been the reason why his brethren took their father's flocks from Hebron, where they seem to have settled for some time, and travelled to Shechem where Jacob owned a parcel of land.

The record does not tell us that they made this move on the instructions of their father and it is not unreasonable to assume that they did so on their own initiative. Shechem was fifty miles (80 km) north of Hebron and it is difficult to disassociate their actions from the situation within the family and the burning resentment that they felt towards Joseph.

Given the distance they had travelled and possibly the time they had been away we can appreciate the anxiety that Jacob would have felt, and who better to send to enquire after their welfare and the condition of the flock than Joseph?

A simple question
Of course when Joseph arrived in Shechem his brethren were not to be found for they had moved to Dothan,

which was approximately twenty miles (32 km) further north. Their failure to communicate with their father regarding their health and safety and their decision to move from Shechem is perhaps an indication of that sense of estrangement that existed within the family. We can well imagine the bewilderment that Joseph felt. Where were they? The whole land lay before him and surely he would eventually have determined to return home to his father with the news that they were not there, and he knew not where they had gone. But God always has the right man in the right place at the right time.

So as he wandered in the open countryside a man met him who asked, "What seekest thou?" (Genesis 37:15). This was a simple, straightforward question, yet when we reflect upon it the whole purpose of God is seen to rest on this and Joseph's reaction to it. If he had not met the man (was he an angel?) then almost certainly Joseph would have returned home to his father and the whole series of events recorded in the latter chapters of Genesis would not have taken place. We know that the purpose of God cannot fail and that ultimately whatever choices men may make His will must prevail. Nevertheless, viewed purely from a human perspective, if Joseph had not been told that his brethren had gone to Dothan, he would not have been sold into slavery in Egypt; he would not have languished for years in the prison house or been exalted by Pharaoh; Israel would not have gone down into Egypt; and there would have been no Passover deliverance.

All this, of course, is quite hypothetical yet surely it teaches us that sometimes the mighty purposes of God are carried forward by events that in themselves are of little significance.

God was with him

Joseph went to Dothan, and his brethren had obviously been thinking about him and the situation in Jacob's household, for resentment still smouldered and festered in their hearts. Their immediate response when they saw his approach was to conspire to kill him and they muttered one to the other, "Behold, this dreamer cometh (Genesis 37:19)".

When Stephen made his defence before the Sanhedrin he referred to these events concerning Joseph and his brethren to demonstrate that the God of Israel could not be confined by the borders of the land they occupied. His power and His purpose extended throughout the earth. He reminds them that:

"The patriarchs, moved with envy, sold Joseph into Egypt: but God was with him, and delivered him out of all his afflictions, and gave him favour and wisdom in the sight of Pharaoh king of Egypt; and he made him governor over Egypt and all his house."

(Acts 7:9,10)

"But God was with him". In those few words Stephen encapsulates the whole record of Genesis chapter 39. For there it is recorded on five separate occasions that God was with Joseph, blessing him so that he prospered in all his ways:

"And the LORD was with Joseph, and he was a prosperous man ... And his master saw that the LORD was with him, and that the LORD made all that he did to prosper in his hand." (verses 2,3)

"But the LORD was with Joseph, and shewed him mercy, and gave him favour in the sight of the keeper of the prison." (verse 21)

"Because the LORD was with him, and that which he did, the LORD made it to prosper." (verse 23)

Joseph's faith

Throughout all the things that he suffered Joseph maintained his belief in God's word and the confidence that ultimately God would deliver him. We might wonder whether, sometimes in all those long years of imprisonment, he pondered what might have been if he had not met the man who asked him, "What seekest thou?" – if, instead, he had returned home to his father.

35

It is a measure of his great spiritual insight and the amazing faith that sustained him, that when eventually he was reunited with his brethren he was able to declare:

"And God sent me before you to preserve you a posterity in the earth, and to save your lives by a great deliverance. So now it was not you that sent me hither, but God." (Genesis 45:7,8)

It is with the benefit of hindsight that we can appreciate the wonderful train of events set in motion by that simple question and Joseph's response to it. It teaches us much about the hand of God in human affairs, and with the apostle we can declare:

"O the depth of the riches both of the wisdom and knowledge of God! How unsearchable are his judgments, and his ways past finding out! For who hath known the mind of the Lord? Or who hath been his counsellor? Or who hath first given to him, and it shall be recompensed unto him again? For of him, and through him, and to him, are all things: to whom be glory for ever. Amen." (Romans 11:33-36)

8

"THE AMEN"

MOST people imagine that the use of the word 'amen' at the end of a prayer signifies 'the end'. Others with more insight have expressed the meaning of the word as 'so be it'. The real significance is deeper still, for 'amen' is a transliteration from the Hebrew and any study of the word must begin therefore in the Old Testament.

The lexicons tell us that there are as many as twelve closely related words that come from the one root 'amen'. To gain an insight into the meanings associated with these words we can divide them into three main categories:

1. To do with building: meaning to prop, to stay, to support, to found, to build up.
2. To do with God: meaning faithfulness, fidelity, truth.
3. To do with God's people: meaning to be faithful, to believe, to trust, to put confidence in.

A brief survey of some of the related words will give an insight into the associations of the word 'amen':

"The testimony of the LORD is sure (i.e., 'amen')."
(Psalm 19:7)

"And thy kingdom shall be established (shall be 'amen') for ever before thee." (2 Samuel 7:16)

"My covenant shall stand fast (be 'amen') with him." (Psalm 89:28)

"I will make an everlasting covenant with you, even the sure (the 'amen') mercies of David."
(Isaiah 55:3)

"And he believed ('amen') in the LORD; and he counted it to him for righteousness." (Genesis 15:6)

37

The last example is particularly significant for the verb 'to believe' is in Hebrew, 'amen'. Thus what God requires of us if we would be counted righteous, that is to have our sins forgiven, is to manifest faith – to show that we recognise God's fidelity and the faithfulness of His word. This we do by saying in effect "amen" to the things that He has written.

The God of truth

The key chapter in the Old Testament is Isaiah 65. We can briefly analyse it thus:

- Verse 1 speaks of the call of the Gentiles. Paul's use of this passage in Romans 10 should be noted ("Esaias is very bold ..." – verses 20,21).
- Verses 2-7 describe how Israel had refused God's overtures of mercy and had remained a rebellious people.
- Verses 8-10 speak of a faithful remnant who would be preserved by God. In this context we might describe them as 'His amen people'.
- Verse 11 reverts to the faithless people of Israel who "prepare a table for that troop (AV margin, Gad) and that furnish the drink offering unto that number (AV margin, Meni)". They had laid on a feast for Gad and Meni who were the heathen gods of luck and fortune.

Thus was expressed their lack of faith in the faithfulness of God; their inability to recognise His fidelity to the covenant that He had made with them.

In the midst of all the uncertainty of human life, the vicissitudes of human experience, they looked to those things that were uncertain and that offered no assurance or confidence. For this reason, whereas God's servants should eat and drink, they would go hungry and thirsty (verses 12,13). On the other hand, "he who (blessed) himself in the earth shall bless himself in the God of truth (literally, 'amen'); and he that sweareth in the earth shall swear by the God of truth ('amen')" (verse 16). They will do so because God has shown His fidelity and revealed Himself by His acts to be the God of the Amen. "For, behold, I create new heavens and a new earth: and the former shall not be remembered, nor come into mind" (verse 17).

Thus all that God has spoken will be consummated in the Amen, His actions being the ultimate vindication of the fidelity of His words.

The New Testament

We turn now to the New Testament and find that the word 'amen' carried over into the Greek text, occurs in almost every book.

The Lord Jesus himself is described as "the faithful witness" (Revelation 1:5). The words are a quotation from Psalm 89 where the moon is described in relation to God's covenant with David as "a faithful (literally, 'an amen') witness in heaven" (verse 37).

He was "the Word made flesh"; hence we might also say that he was faithfulness incarnate, for in him all the promises of God met and through him will find their ultimate fulfilment. In the Epistle to the Romans, the Apostle Paul writes concerning him:

"Now I say that Jesus Christ was a minister of the circumcision for the truth of God, to confirm the promises made unto the fathers."   (Romans 15:8)

The word rendered "truth" has the following associations: stability, trust, certainty, faithful, right and sure – in other words, all the qualities that we have seen associated with the word 'amen'. In the Lord Jesus all the truth of God, all His promises have been confirmed. They have been made sure through his sacrifice and resurrection from the dead. In the words of the epistle to the Hebrews, it is "through the blood of the everlasting covenant" (13:20). So the apostle could write again:

"For all the promises of God in him are yea, and in him Amen, unto the glory of God by us."

(2 Corinthians 1:20)

The Apocalypse

In the Apocalypse the idea of the faithfulness of God is emphasised very strongly. Note for instance that the three titles used of the Lord Jesus Christ in chapter 1 – "the faithful witness, the first begotten of the dead, and the prince of the kings of the earth" (verse 5) – are all drawn from Psalm 89, the theme of which is God's faithfulness to the covenant that He made with David (see verses 1,2,3,5,8,17). The idea is carried over into the message to the seven ecclesias of Asia. Thus the message to Philadelphia is from "he that is holy, he that is true" (Revelation 3:7) and the promise to "him that overcometh" is that he will become "a pillar in the temple of my God" (verse 12). The reference carries us back to the temple built by Solomon and perhaps to the two pillars of brass, Jachin and Boaz in particular. The interesting fact, however, that links with our opening summary is the connection that the Hebrew word 'amen' had with building. The word translated "pillar", which means literally 'to support, to uphold' is in the Old Testament this very word 'amen', and the promise is one of assurance of everlasting stability in God's spiritual house, for those so blessed shall "go no more out".

It remains to note that to the ecclesia at Laodicea the Lord addresses himself in a direct allusion to Isaiah 65, as "the Amen, the faithful and true witness" (3:14).

All our thoughts are perhaps caught up and expressed by the words of our hymn 174, written by Brother David Brown and included in *The Golden Harp*, our community's first Hymn Book in 1864:

Speed on, O God, the hour when, free from sin,
We'll rise, Thy sons of power, glorious within:
And, with the Christ confest,
Blessing and ever blest,
Rule o'er the earth at rest in the Amen.

9

THE MAN NEHEMIAH

NEHEMIAH is one of the great Old Testament characters and one of the few of whom there is no recorded sin. He was a man of decision and action who had no time for apathy and lethargy but, seeing a work to be done, led by example. He had an intense devotion to his God, a love for Jerusalem, His city, and an abiding concern for his brethren, the people of Israel.

His self-sacrifice

Nehemiah, although a stranger in a strange land, held a responsible position in the court of the king. As cupbearer he would have been a trusted official who ministered personally to the sovereign. With his responsibilities there came also the comfort and advantages that would be associated with the royal palace of an absolute monarch. Above all things, because of his reliability and faithful service to the king, there would have been security in his environment.

Nevertheless, when he heard of the plight of his brethren who had returned to the land and the state of disrepair of the walls and gates of Jerusalem, his heart was stirred and he determined to approach the king. Although there was some peril for him in this, he wanted permission to travel to Jerusalem to do what he could to remedy the situation (Nehemiah 1:2,3; 2:1-4). To take such action required a lack of concern for his own personal safety and a willingness to sacrifice all his security and comfort for the hardship and privation that the work at Jerusalem involved. He was not lacking in that spirit of self-denial demanded by the task ahead.

His humility

When Nehemiah hears the news from Jerusalem, his reaction gives a remarkable insight into the spirit of the man:

> "When I heard these words, I sat down and wept, and mourned certain days, and fasted, and prayed before the God of heaven." (1:4)

He did not adopt a 'holier than thou' attitude. He did not say, "How could they have let things get so bad?" But in his prayer, devoid of any pride and arrogance, he associated himself with the sins of his people:

> "We have sinned against thee: both I and my father's house have sinned. We have dealt very corruptly against thee." (1:6,7)

Although he was not personally responsible for the situation at Jerusalem, he associated himself with his people in the guilt; he acknowledged it as a corporate responsibility. He did not say, "It is nothing to do with me", but he recognised that they all belonged to the family of God and as such shared a common responsibility. We see the same attitude in Daniel (9:3-19) and other men of God and it is a spirit we do well to emulate in our ecclesial life. If there are things wrong within the brotherhood we cannot say, "Nothing to do with me", for there is a corporate responsibility.

A man of the word

The word of God was powerful in Nehemiah's life. If we look for instance at his prayer in Nehemiah chapter 1 and analyse just a few verses, we find that his petitions are built upon the things that God had written – through Moses in particular.

> "The great and terrible God, that keepeth covenant and mercy ..." (verse 5 – see Deuteronomy 7:12,21)

> "If ye transgress, I will scatter you abroad among the nations."
> (verse 8 – see Leviticus 26:33, Deuteronomy 4:27)

> "But if ye turn unto me ..."
> (verse 9 – see Deuteronomy 4:29)

"Though there were of you cast out unto the uttermost part of the heaven, yet will I gather them from thence." (verse 9 – see Deuteronomy 30:1-5)

"The place that I have chosen to set my name there." (verse 9 – see Deuteronomy 12:5)

It is a very brief survey, but it indicates that he was a 'man of the word' – it was a living power in his heart.

His example

Nehemiah was not a man who simply made decisions, or gave instructions for others to carry out. One of his outstanding characteristics was that he led from the front. In the face of opposition from the people round about, he showed courage and faith in God and was a constant source of encouragement to his brethren:

"In what place therefore ye hear the sound of the trumpet, resort ye thither unto us: our God shall fight for us. So we laboured in the work ... So neither I, nor my brethren ... none of us put off our clothes, saving that every one put them off for washing." (4:20-23)

It was not just in the work of building, however, that he was a shining example. It is not always appreciated that Nehemiah held the office of governor and could therefore speak with a certain authority. It appears that many of the poor of the people had been cruelly oppressed by their richer brethren. Because of their need for food they had mortgaged their lands, vineyards and houses and were now unable to redeem their possessions and were in virtual bondage to the rich and powerful (5:1-5). Nehemiah says:

"I was very angry when I heard their cry ... Then I consulted with myself, and I rebuked the nobles, and the rulers." (verses 6,7)

The result was that they hearkened to the words of Nehemiah and released their brethren from their debts.

The reason, however, why he could speak with such authority was because of his own personal example. During the course of the first of his two visits to Jerusalem, a period of twelve years, he had not eaten the bread of the governor. Previously governors had exacted bread, wine and money from the people to maintain their position, and their servants had exercised unjust authority over the people. Nehemiah says, "So did not I, because of the fear of God" (verse 15). He did not pursue his own interests, he bought no land but he and his servants continued with the work in hand. But over and above all this, at his own expense, he provided meat and wine. Daily, a hundred-and-fifty Jews and others who were round about (Gentiles) sat at his table and were succoured. What a man! "Yet for all this required not I the bread of the governor, because the bondage was heavy upon this people" (verse 18).

His consciousness of God

In all that he did, Nehemiah was aware that it was God's work and that He would bring it to a successful conclusion. There were no miracles, but through prayer and recognition of His providential hand there was constant acknowledgement of God's help and activity amongst them. For example:

- "Prosper, I pray thee, thy servant this day" (1:11)
- "So I prayed to the God of heaven" (2:4)
- "Then I told them of the hand of my God which was good upon me" (2:18)
- "The God of heaven, he will prosper us" (2:20)
- "Hear, O our God; for we are despised … So built we the wall" (4:4-6)
- "Nevertheless we made our prayer unto our God (4:9)
- "Our God shall fight for us" (4:20)

There was no open manifestation of God's power, nevertheless it was a miracle, for in fifty-two days the work was finished and even their astonished enemies could see that this was wrought of their God (6:15,16).

What better epitaph could a man have?

"Think upon me, O my God, for good, according to all that I have done for this people." (5:19)

10

"IT WAS NIGHT"

ONE of the great themes in John's Gospel is the conflict between light and darkness. The scene is set in the prologue to the Gospel (1:1-14) where the principles developed in a variety of ways through the pages of the record are first emphasised. Verses 4 and 5 introduce the theme of light and darkness and the punctuation and rendering of the RV text (with margin) help to establish the message of these verses:

"That which hath been made was life in him; and the life was the light of men. And the light shineth in the darkness; and the darkness overcame it not".

All life has its source in God but the life which God gives to man, although similar naturally to that which the animal creation has, assumes spiritual and moral qualities in man that are unique to him. Man was made in the image and likeness of God. God is light, perfect and absolute, and ultimately without light there can be no life. So in man, life is equated with light and man's eternal future depends upon the way in which he allows his life to be illuminated by the light of God. The Psalmist writes:

"For with thee is the fountain of life: in thy light shall we see light."   (Psalm 36:9)

It is a fact that in the natural order of things, darkness of itself can never extinguish light. So in the spiritual sphere, the light of the truth has shone throughout human history and the darkness has been unable to overcome it. This conflict now becomes focused in the person of the Lord Jesus Christ and those who opposed him. "The true light, which lighteth every man, was coming into the world" (verse 9 RV, with margin). Note particularly the changes in the

45

punctuation. This makes it clear that it was "the true light" (the Lord Jesus Christ) that was coming into the world and that this light was for every man: not every man without exception, for our own experience of life teaches us that this is not true; rather it is every man without distinction – Jew or Greek, bond or free, male or female. The light of the Gospel is for all: for all, that is, who will receive it. It is the true light – not true as opposed to false, for you cannot have a false light, but true in the sense of real. The light that is in us can be darkness if we have espoused error, but in the very nature of things light and darkness cannot be mixed and the illumination that light gives is intrinsic to its nature. The word rendered "truth" in this passage is used twenty-two times in John's Gospel and always it carries the meaning of the real or the substance as opposed to the type or shadow, the perfect or complete as opposed to that which is incomplete:

"God, who at sundry times and in divers manners spake in times past unto the fathers by the prophets, *hath in these last days spoken unto us by his Son.*"

(Hebrews 1:1,2)

Man's reaction to the light

As the light shines in darkness, so men are judged by their reaction to it:

"He that believeth on him is not condemned: but he that believeth not is condemned already, because he hath not believed in the name of the only begotten Son of God. And this is the condemnation, that light is come into the world and men loved darkness rather than light, because their deeds were evil. For every one that doeth evil hateth the light, neither cometh to the light, lest his deeds should be reproved."

(John 3:18-20)

Men are judged by their reaction to the Lord Jesus and they stand self-condemned it they reject the light that was embodied in him – if, because their works are evil, they hate the light. Such men shrink from the illumination that would show them for what they really

46

are, and by which they would be reproved (literally 'laid bare'). In the development of this theme in his Gospel, John, through the spirit, employs language which describes the natural or physical conditions in which certain events happened but, at the same time, intends us to discern a deeper spiritual significance.

Thus Nicodemus, who came to Jesus by night (3:1,2), is referred to by John in this manner on the other two occasions that he mentions him (7:50; 19:39). Clearly Nicodemus had reasons for coming to the Lord Jesus under the cloak of darkness. He was an influential man, some say the president of the council; he would not show himself openly seeking counsel of Jesus. Like so many, he would hide his belief lest he bring upon himself the ridicule and scorn of his peers. He was a disciple secretly for fear of the Jews, but eventually when the Lord Jesus died on the cross, he was moved to show his esteem for him when he associated himself with Joseph of Arimathaea in making arrangements for his burial. He came out of the shadows into the light. He was prepared to disregard the consequences of his actions that he might be made manifest by the light. Such is the experience of many, but sooner or later they must find the courage to acknowledge the Lord publicly and openly whatever the cost.

Judas was of the night

We have another example in the record concerning Judas Iscariot:

> "And after the sop Satan entered into him. Then said Jesus unto him, That thou doest, do quickly … He then having received the sop went immediately out: and it was night." (John 13:27-30)

The words are pregnant with significance. Of course it was night literally, but also it had a deep spiritual significance, for Judas was of the night. He could not stand in the presence of the Lord Jesus, that divine illumination that shone into his heart, and revealed him for what he really was. So he went out from Jesus where the light was, into the gathering gloom – that darkness that was to lay hold on him and envelop him for ever.

It was winter

Similarly John uses the season of the year, the climatic conditions, to express a like truth in chapter 10:

> "And it was at Jerusalem the feast of dedication, and it was winter." (verse 22)

The scriptures do not waste words. Of course it was literally winter, but again it is a device to describe a great spiritual truth for "this was their hour, and the power of darkness". It was winter when the days became shorter and the nights grew longer, when the chill and biting winds blew and the storm clouds gathered. So as Gethsemane and the cross drew nearer, as the clouds of adversity began to envelop the Lord and the cold implacable hatred of his enemies grew more intense, John sums up these circumstances with that cryptic comment, "It was winter".

That this is the significance of the phrase is made even clearer when we remember the context of the chapter with its teaching of the Good Shepherd. The marginal references will show how marked are the points of connection between the words of the Lord Jesus and Ezekiel 34. This connection is beyond dispute. How revealing then are the words of the prophet:

> "As a shepherd seeketh out his flock in the day that he is among the sheep that are scattered; so will I seek out my sheep, and will deliver them out of all places where they have been scattered in the cloudy and dark day." (Ezekiel 34:12)

Truly the shepherd would be smitten and the sheep scattered in that day when the power of darkness would appear to have prevailed. But the light shone and the darkness overcame it not. Thus the Lord overcame sin and was raised to life again that he might gather unto himself his sheep who hear his voice.

The brook Kidron

We look briefly at one final example: "When Jesus had spoken these words, he went forth with his disciples over the brook Kidron, where was a garden" (John 18:1, RV). The RV margin renders the word "brook", "*ravine*, Gr. *winter-torrent*", for it was a rocky defile down which, in winter, the waters would rush in a torrent. The words of the Psalmist come to mind: "I am come into deep waters, where the floods overflow me" (Psalm 69:2). Such passages must surely have been the Lord's meditation as he traversed the winter torrent Kidron, and the word Kidron itself adds to the picture for it means 'blackness'. How appropriate this was to describe the ordeal that lay before the Lord Jesus. Hundreds of years previously, his forbear David had trodden the same path when his son Absalom had rebelled against him. He had turned his face towards the wilderness (2 Samuel 15:23). He had gone in faith, knowing that nothing could frustrate the covenant that God had made with him. So eventually he came again to his throne at Jerusalem. Thus, the Lord Jesus, in faith, went forth in similar confidence, knowing that like David he too would come again, for the grave could not hold him and God would raise him up again.

Conclusion

The light still shines into the darkness and the challenge of the Lord Jesus Christ remains as potent as ever. By our works we show whether we are of the light or the darkness. He who reflects the light of the knowledge of the glory of God, who hath shined into our hearts, still says to whomsoever will hear:

"I am the light of the world: he that followeth me shall not walk in darkness, but shall have the light of life." (John 8:12)

11

"THROUGH MUCH TRIBULATION"

AS Paul and Barnabas approached the end of the first missionary journey they came again to Lystra, Iconium and Antioch, "confirming the souls of the disciples, and exhorting them to continue in the faith, and that we must through much tribulation enter into the kingdom of God" (Acts 14:21,22). Of the Greek word translated "tribulation", *Vine's Expository Dictionary* tells us that it has reference to "pressure of circumstances and the antagonism of persons".

We readily appreciate that the antagonism of persons relates to the persecution that belief in the Gospel can sometimes bring. We know that this was a very real problem for many of our first century brethren and sisters. Equally we know that for most of us, persecution is not a great problem. Accepting therefore the truth of the apostle's words we must look in our lives at the pressure of circumstances in particular.

What does it mean to live under pressure? We might say that it refers to the affliction, anguish, trouble that we all experience in our daily lives. In short, every kind of ill to which humankind is heir. But therein lies the problem for us. For what is different in our experience from that of our contemporaries with whom we rub shoulders day by day? We are all subject to sickness, disease, anxiety, grief – for this is the common legacy of our human nature. How then do we enter the kingdom "through much tribulation"?

The Lord Jesus said:

> "Strive to enter in at the strait gate: for many, I say unto you, will seek to enter in, and shall not be able."
> (Luke 13:24)

The word "strive" means literally 'to agonise' and it helps us to appreciate the effort that is needed to live the life to which God has called us. The word "strait" carries the idea of compression and again speaks to us unerringly of the difficulty of travelling that narrow path that leads to God's kingdom. The gate is strait and the path narrow because God has made it so. He requires us to submit to the discipline that He has imposed. In which way therefore, given our shared experiences with our fellow men, is this tribulation, this pressure of circumstances, worked out in our lives?

Illustrations from the word

Consider the example of Abraham and Sarah. Naturally speaking, they must have longed for a child. In this respect they were no different from any other couple who long for a child. However, what made the difference was the word of God. Faith was introduced into the situation and the promise that God had given made them different from all others. For twenty-five long years they waited and throughout that time there must have been occasions when they experienced anxiety and uncertainty. Nevertheless, they "staggered not at the promise of God through unbelief; but were strong in faith, giving glory to God; and being fully persuaded that, what he had promised, he was able also to perform" (Romans 4:20,21).

Think also of Joseph. Here we have an individual who suffered a great deal. He was sold by his brethren and taken into the land of Egypt. In the house of Potiphar it might be said, to use a modern idiom, that he had landed on his feet. Here, however, as a result of the actions of a malevolent woman he was thrust into prison and although innocent of any crime suffered cruelly. Scripture does not tell us how long Joseph was in prison but we know that he was seventeen when his brothers sold him into Egypt, and thirty when he was elevated in the kingdom by Pharaoh. It is not unreasonable therefore to presume that he was incarcerated in that prison for approximately ten years.

Now Joseph is not the only person who has been imprisoned unjustly. In recent times we have seen a spate of 'miscarriages of justice' and down through the centuries there must have been countless examples of people who were punished for crimes of which they were completely innocent. Yet Joseph was different. God had revealed to him through his dreams that he would be exalted above his brethren and that a time would come when they would bow themselves before him. We can imagine that this would have been a source of comfort to him in those long years of confinement. It gave him hope. But at the same time what doubts and uncertainties must have assailed him, for the future must have appeared very bleak to this righteous man.

The Psalmist gives us a proper perspective on his experiences:

"He sent a man before them, even Joseph, who was sold for a servant: whose feet they hurt with fetters: he was laid in iron: until the time that his word came: the word of the LORD tried him."   (Psalm 105:17-19)

As with Abraham and Sarah, what made the difference was the word of God. By the word that God had spoken Joseph was put to the test. It does not take a lot of imagination to appreciate the wrestling of heart that he must have experienced in those long years of imprisonment. As one writer has put it, "the iron entered his soul".

The word in our lives

Similarly it is the word of God that makes the difference in the experiences that we share with our fellow men. As the experiences of godly men and women of old were not unique in themselves, so our participation in the common lot of all men is transformed by the influence of the word of God in our lives. Here is a pressure of circumstance of which the worldly-minded man knows nothing. In all the vicissitudes of life that word transforms our perception of events and produces a faith in God's promises that brings also, because of the nature we bear, a continuous conflict between the flesh and the spirit. Like Abraham and Joseph we know that God is at work in our lives. The consciousness of His presence is something that only constant meditation upon the word of God can produce. Inevitably there will be days of darkness and adversity and with them an inner conflict of which the godless man is ignorant.

Suffering through temptation

The Lord Jesus is the supreme example. It is recorded of him:

> "For in that he himself has suffered being tempted, he is able to succour them that are tempted."
>
> (Hebrews 2:18)

Our minds wrestle to understand fully that inner conflict that he experienced in his temptations. Here was a man who could read the Old Testament scriptures as no other. They described not only the path he must tread in life but also his own innermost longings and desires. He knew that if he should sin there would be no life, not just for himself, but for any man. This is the burden that he carried throughout his life, and as he began his ministry and the final crisis drew closer how the pressure of responsibility that lay upon him must have increased.

It is not always appreciated that the scriptures do not place a great emphasis upon the physical sufferings of the Lord Jesus. They do not minimise them but imagine how men might have described them, sparing us no gory detail. It is surely a mark of inspiration that there is an economy of language in the description of the things that he endured. For instance:

> "And when they were come to the place, which is called Calvary, there they crucified him."
>
> (Luke 23:33)

Compare these brief words with the Lord's mental agony in Gethsemane:

> "And he was withdrawn from them about a stone's cast, and kneeled down, and prayed, saying, Father, if

thou be willing, remove this cup from me: nevertheless not my will, but thine, be done. And there appeared an angel unto him from heaven, strengthening him. And being in an agony he prayed more earnestly: and his sweat was as it were great drops of blood falling down to the ground."

(Luke 22:41-44)

Similarly the writer to the Hebrews expresses in a most poignant fashion the inner conflict that the Lord Jesus experienced:

"Who in the days of his flesh, when he had offered up prayers and supplications, with strong crying and tears unto him that was able to save him from death, and was heard in that he feared. Though he were a Son, yet learned he obedience by the things which he suffered." (Hebrews 5:7,8)

Taking up our cross

We need to appreciate that the Lord's suffering, culminating in his painful experiences at the hands of the Jews and Pilate, and his subsequent death on the cross was preceded by a whole lifetime of wrestling with the nature he bore. Just as the Lord's temptations were an integral part of his sufferings, we also suffer being tempted. Because of the influence of the word of God in our lives we have to take up our cross and follow him. We are called to a life of self-sacrifice and self-denial that demands continuous effort and commitment in the daily conflict with our natural tendencies. Herein lies the "much tribulation" through which we enter the kingdom of God. We must strive to live the life that was manifested in the Lord Jesus Christ. If we do, then we can say with the Apostle Paul: "I am crucified with Christ" (Galatians 2:20); "I die daily" (1 Corinthians 15:31).

To know now the fellowship of the Lord's sufferings, to experience also the succour that he offers to us in all our trials and temptations, is to know also the confidence that, by God's grace, we will be numbered amongst the multitude of the redeemed which come out of "great tribulation", having "washed their robes and made them white in the blood of the Lamb" (Revelation 7:14).

12

REFLECTIONS ON 3 JOHN

IN no sense is this study to be regarded as an exposition of this short epistle. Rather it is intended to emphasise some of the lessons that we can learn from a consideration of its exhortational content. 3 John is a short personal letter addressed to an individual known as Gaius. This is one of the most common of Roman names. It is found on four other occasions in the New Testament, but there is no evidence to connect the person addressed in this epistle with any of these. What do we find that is striking about this letter? Well, apart from the reference to Diotrephes (verse 9), surely it is the sheer ordinariness of it. There is nothing exceptional about it, but it speaks of the average everyday life of a believer. It has to do with the day to day practice of living the Truth. In this respect we can all relate to it, especially as it comes from the pen of the beloved Apostle John. He speaks with a quiet authority and conviction born of long years of dedication to the Lord Jesus Christ and commitment to the work that had been entrusted to him.

Gaius the Beloved

"The elder unto Gaius the beloved, whom I love in truth."   (verse 1, RV)

The reference to this man as "the beloved" is an indication of the esteem in which he was held by his fellow brethren and sisters. By his way of life he commended himself to all who knew him and this John recognised and acknowledged. The Greek word is, of course, derived from the word *agape* and speaks not of natural love and affection, although that might well have existed, but of that spiritual bond that transcends all fleshly emotions.

As brethren and sisters in the Lord Jesus Christ we are all different. With some we have a natural affinity; with others, perhaps, there is no inclination to ordinary human attraction. But we are not called to like one another but to love each other as ourselves. Hence the bond that binds us together should be stronger than any natural emotion, for the hope that holds us together in fellowship is the common salvation that we share in the Lord Jesus Christ.

Love in truth

Thus when John continues – "whom I love in truth" – he is not repeating the emphasis of the word "beloved", but is expressing his own conviction that Gaius was worthy of the respect in which he was held. Notice the absence of the definite article. John is speaking of the genuineness of his own love. He associates himself with the general opinion regarding this man and speaks of the reality of his own feelings concerning him. In effect John says, 'I speak from the heart'.

He had used similar language in his first epistle:

"My little children, let us not love in word, neither with the tongue; but in deed and truth."   (3:18, RV)

Notice that "word" is contrasted with "deed" and "tongue" with "truth". Is this merely repetition for emphasis? By no means! It is possible to look on suffering and hardship experienced by our brethren and sisters and to feel a genuine sense of concern. We can share the general expressions of anxiety for the circumstances in which they find themselves. Somehow, however, the words we speak are never translated into deeds. Our sense of sorrow is genuine enough, but in the busy lives we live there is always so much to do and our concern is not translated into action.

However, when the apostle contrasts the tongue with truth he is carrying us a step further. Now he is describing words that are not genuine; words that have

57

no substance in truth; empty words that have no real meaning. They are not spoken from the heart but they are said because one knows what ought to be said; because we would not have others think anything but well of us. In reality, to love with the tongue and not in truth is to practise hypocrisy.

Prosperity and health

On three other occasions in the epistle, John expresses his esteem for Gaius by addressing him as "beloved" (verses 2, 5, and 11):

> "Beloved, I pray that in all things thou mayest prosper and be in health, even as thy soul prospereth." (verse 2)

Clearly it is not spiritual health and prosperity that John prays for. That Gaius is living his life in the Truth successfully John has no doubt. He had heard again and again of his faithfulness from the brethren who visited him. What then did John long for? We cannot imagine that it was for material prosperity in this world's goods. Surely what John was praying for was God's blessing on life. The word translated "prosper" means 'to help on the road; to succeed in reaching' (*Strong's Concordance*). So it was John's desire that he would be blessed with health and success to live in all its fulness that life to which he had been called in Christ – a life of service and commitment unhindered by distressing circumstances and human weakness.

Perhaps this is an aspect of the concern that we should feel for one another that we do not think about enough. It is possible that Gaius had not been in the best of health but the force of the exhortation is not affected. We too should not neglect to pray for all those amongst us who carry the burden of responsibility in our ecclesial life. No one is indispensable but nevertheless we need to show our appreciation of the fact that their labours are recognised and that if, through the circumstances of life, they should be prevented from continuing in them, then that would be detrimental to us and the work of the Truth generally.

The exhortation, of course, is there for everyone. While health and strength remain we should all seek to be busy in the Lord's work and grasp the opportunities that life presents.

John's joy

Having thus prayed for Gaius to be blessed with health and opportunity to continue in his labours, John now expresses the joy he feels in hearing of the spiritual quality of his life:

> "For I rejoiced greatly, when the brethren came and testified of the truth that is in thee, even as thou walkest in the truth. I have no greater joy than to hear that my children walk in truth."   (verses 3,4)

Do we rejoice together in the spiritual life that we share? Do we take an interest in each other's welfare, or are we more concerned with finding fault with our fellow labourers? We all need encouragement and this short letter is full of it. To Gaius he says: 'You are doing well. Your spiritual life is prospering. Keep it up and don't be distracted by the influence of evil men. Continue to walk in that way which you have chosen'.

Continuing in well-doing is of vital importance to us all. To the ecclesia at Thessalonica Paul wrote:

> "And the Lord make you to increase and abound in love one toward another, and toward all men, even as we do toward you."   (1 Thessalonians 3:12)

> "… as ye have received of us how ye ought to walk and to please God, so ye would abound more and more."   (4:1)

Life in the Truth can never stand still. There never comes a time when we can say, 'I have done enough'. Old age, health, or the buffeting of life might make it impossible for us to continue in the work we were once engaged in. However, as the circumstances of life change so we must look for new avenues of service and, if we can do nothing else, we can still pray for those who are working actively in God's vineyard.

Hospitality to the brethren

One of the things for which John particularly commends Gaius is the hospitality that he showed both to the brethren and to strangers:

> "Beloved, thou doest a faithful work in whatsoever thou doest toward them that are brethren and strangers withal; who bare witness to thy love before the church: whom thou wilt do well to set forward on their journey worthily of God: because that for the sake of the Name they went forth, taking nothing of the Gentiles. We therefore ought to welcome such, that we may be fellow-workers with the truth."
>
> (3 John 5-8, RV)

We believe it would be true to say that, generally speaking, the hospitality we show is a characteristic of our community that sets us apart from all others. We open our homes to campaigners, speakers, students, casual visitors on holiday or business. Whatever our faults, we might say that this is not one. Nevertheless there is a lesson to be learned.

We need to remember that the social structure of life in the first century was quite different from ours. Those who came were almost always those who were engaged in the Lord's work. In a very real sense Gaius was helping them in their labours. Notice the contrast in the second epistle:

> "If there come any unto you, and bring not this doctrine, receive him not into your house, neither bid him God speed: for he that biddeth him God speed is partaker of his evil deeds." (2 John 10,11)

Fellow workers

The work which Gaius performed was in every sense that of a "fellow worker with the truth". Of course the hospitality that we show can often be described in those terms, but not always. Sometimes it can be no more than a sharing of each other's company on a social level – not that there is anything wrong with that, unless we restrict our hospitality to merely social exchanges.

However, what John is speaking of is the commitment that we should have to use all that we possess in the Lord's service. To carry the thought a little further, we are united together in a common bond. A great work has been committed to our trust. Do we then show this in our support for those who labour in the Gospel? Not just in the hospitality we show but also in giving financial help, in praying for the work to be undertaken and, when the activities are organised by our own ecclesia, by our unstinting endeavour to support the work in whatever way possible.

It is of vital importance that we work together and do not seek to express our own individuality. We must not absorb ourselves in things that spring from our own initiative to the detriment of ecclesially organised events. This would be a little like the spirit of Diotrephes who loved to have the pre-eminence (3 John 9). He wanted his own way. He was determined by the force of his personality to impose his will on his brethren and sisters. He refused even to welcome the apostle, and showed him no hospitality. We need always to remember that we are fellow workers together. As Peter counselled:

"Be ye all of one mind (literally 'unanimous, concordant'), compassionate, loving as brethren."

(1 Peter 3:8)

Paul spoke of our being –

"labourers together with God." (1 Corinthians 3:9)

Conclusion

So from this short personal letter we have an insight into the daily life of a committed disciple. In his own quiet way he served his Lord with all his heart and left an example of all that the Lord Jesus should mean to us in our daily walk to the kingdom of God.

13

TIMOTHY – A MODEL DISCIPLE

W E are first introduced to the young man Timothy when Paul, accompanied by Silas, came for the second time to Derbe and Lystra (Acts 16:1). Here they find Timothy, whose mother was a Jew and a believer, whereas his father was a Greek.

At Lystra and Iconium, Timothy had already commended himself to the brethren by his manner of life. The AV says that "he was well reported of" (verse 2). The Greek word means 'witness' and is derived from the word used when the Lord Jesus told the disciples that they should be witnesses unto him (Acts 1:8). In other words, Timothy, by his behaviour, was a testimony to the things he believed. He was a living witness unto the Lord Jesus, to whom he had committed his life.

Although the record is silent at this point, one wonders whether Paul had been acquainted with this family previously. His recollection of the faith of Timothy's grandmother Lois and his mother Eunice (2 Timothy 1:5) suggests that he did know them and had perhaps known Timothy from a little child (3:15). Indeed the closeness of the association might suggest that Paul had been a significant influence on Timothy's early life and development, possibly during the years that Paul had spent in Tarsus after his conversion.

The fact that there is no mention of the family on his first visit to these cities with Barnabas (Acts 14) might suggest that they had only moved there in the intervening period. Alternatively, it might be that it was on this first visit that Timothy embraced the faith, being influenced by the example of the Apostle Paul who, as a consequence of the hatred of the Jews at Antioch and Iconium, was stoned at Lystra and presumed dead. Certainly it must have made a profound impression on those disciples (and others) who gathered around Paul when he rose up and entered again into the city (verses 19,20).

Is this implied by Paul's words to Timothy?

"But thou hast fully known my doctrine, manner of life, purpose, faith, longsuffering, charity, patience, persecutions, afflictions, which came unto me at Antioch, at Iconium, at Lystra; what persecutions I endured: but out of them all the Lord delivered me."
(2 Timothy 3:10,11)

If indeed it was Paul's teaching and example at this time that brought Timothy to commit himself in faith to the Lord Jesus, then we can well understand how by influencing him in his formative years and bringing him eventually to baptism, Paul should regard Timothy as his "son in the faith".

"My own son in the faith"

Paul's affection for Timothy is something that goes beyond the normal relationship that one would expect to exist between brethren. Both the epistles written to him are testimonies to Paul's love and concern for him and three passages in particular emphasise the closeness of their relationship.

In his first epistle, Paul addresses Timothy as "my true child in faith" (1:2, RV). The word "child" conveys the idea of special affection as a natural father might show towards his son. The word "true" indicates that a real resemblance existed between them – not a physical likeness as with a natural relationship, but a spiritual resemblance to his father in Christ. Similarly in the second epistle, Paul describes him as "my beloved child" (1:2, RV) and expresses his longing to see Timothy, being mindful of the tears shed because of their enforced separation (verses 3,4). Paul also commends Timothy to the Philippians:

"But I trust in the Lord Jesus to send Timotheus shortly unto you, that I also may be of good comfort, when I know your state. For I have no man likeminded (AV margin, "so dear unto me"), who will naturally care for your state. For all seek their own, not the things which are Jesus Christ's. But ye know the proof of him, that, as a son with the father, he hath served with me in the gospel."   (2:19-22)

What a remarkable young man he was! Timothy did not seek honour for himself. He was not motivated by self-interest, but "as a child serves the father" (literally translated) he laboured with Paul in the Gospel.

Through much of Paul's missionary work, Timothy was his trusted companion. He was with Paul at Philippi (Acts 16). He was there with Silas through all the privations Paul suffered at Corinth and also at Ephesus (Acts 18:5; 19:21,22), and when Paul was in prison in Rome, Timothy was there, ministering to the apostle's needs and assisting him in the work (Colossians 1:1; Philippians 1:1). He was associated with epistles that the apostle sent to the ecclesias he had established (1 and 2 Thessalonians, 2 Corinthians, Colossians and Philippians); also the letter to Philemon. Again he was with Paul when he penned the epistle to the Romans (16:21). When the apostle was approaching the end of his life, it was Timothy he longed to see (2 Timothy 1:4) and whom he urged to give all diligence to come to him and to bring those necessary things for the ministry (4:9,13).

Timothy's character

Timothy was a true disciple of the Lord Jesus Christ. He could be trusted implicitly for he was a man of integrity. There was no one so close to Paul as Timothy. He could be sent anywhere and was always willing to go. The message was as safe with him as if Paul had delivered it himself. He was his trusted representative at Thessalonica (1 Thessalonians 3:6), at Corinth (1 Corinthians 4:17) and at Philippi (Philippians 2:19).

It is interesting therefore to observe that he was not a forceful personality. He did not seek to project himself or to impose himself upon others. Timothy was not an

64

extrovert, but by nature a rather shy and retiring individual. He was in fact a man who, without support and guidance, might be inclined to let others take advantage of him. The evidence is mainly in the epistles that Paul addressed to him and also suggested by other factors that can be inferred from the record in Acts.

It is interesting to reflect that although Timothy was with Paul and Silas in Philippi, he is not mentioned in the confrontation they had with the authorities, nor their subsequent imprisonment (Acts 16). Similarly at Thessalonica, Timothy was with Paul but seems to have escaped the vitriolic hatred of the Jews, and whereas Paul and Silas were forced to move to Berea, there is no mention of Timothy having to do so. Evidently, he was able to remain in Thessalonica to continue supporting the ecclesia there. We wonder whether Paul and Silas were, what we might describe as, "front line preachers", whereas Timothy's work was of a more supportive nature with the newly converted brethren and sisters. This was perhaps a more fitting area of responsibility for his retiring personality.

So in writing to the Corinthians Paul urges:

"Now if Timotheus come, see that he may be with you without fear; for he worketh the work of the Lord, as I also do." (1 Corinthians 16:10)

Similarly in his epistles to Timothy, Paul writes:

"Let no man despise thy youth." (1 Timothy 4:12)

And again:

"Wherefore I put thee in remembrance that thou stir up the gift of God, which is in thee by the putting on of my hands. For God hath not given us the spirit of fear; but of power, and of love, and of a sound mind. Be not thou therefore ashamed of the testimony of our Lord, nor of me his prisoner: but be thou partaker of the afflictions of the gospel according to the power of God." (2 Timothy 1:6-8)

The man Timothy stands as an exhortation to us all. He was perhaps not naturally disposed to the responsibilities that were laid upon him. Nevertheless he was able to rise above his natural disabilities and fulfil all his potential in service to his Lord. He was a model disciple and each one of us can learn from his example. Whatever our talents we can, by God's grace, rise above our natural weaknesses and serve our Lord Jesus to the fullness of our ability.

14

"HERE WE HAVE NO CONTINUING CITY"

THE eleventh chapter of the epistle to the Hebrews presents us with a series of examples of men and women who lived by faith. The context is that of Hebrew believers who were in danger of defecting from their allegiance to the Lord Jesus Christ and returning to the weak and beggarly elements of the Law from which they had been delivered. It is almost certain that the epistle was written in the last days of Judah's Commonwealth. The time was fast drawing near when the Mosaic constitution would be finally swept away before the might and power of Rome. It was, perhaps, in a mistaken sense of loyalty to those things which they had been brought up to hold dear, and an affection for that literal city Jerusalem, that their hearts now turned again to them, as they became increasingly aware of the threat they faced.

They were allowing the things that were to pass away (12:27) to blind them to the eternal and abiding things that they had found in the Lord Jesus Christ.

Now we are not Hebrews. We have not been, as they were, brought up under an order of things that we loved and revered. We do not have the same sense of loyalty and devotion to a literal city as they had for the Jerusalem that then was.

Nevertheless, the danger of defection can be just as real for us as it was for them. The world from which we have been delivered can be just as attractive and even more enticing and the things that now are, can capture our hearts and have just as devastating an effect on our faith as those things had on some of them.

Indeed we do not even have to "forsake the assembling of ourselves together" (10:25), for we can cling to the things that now are, while appearing at the same time, to maintain our faith and commitment to the Lord Jesus Christ.

A consideration of some of the "witnesses" (12:1) brought to our attention in Hebrews 11 might help us to see more distinctly the comparison between those things that are to pass away and those things that are eternal.

By faith Noah

"By faith Noah, being warned of God, moved with fear, built an ark to the saving of his house. Whereby he condemned the world and became an heir of the righteousness that is by faith."   (Hebrews 11:7)

It is surprising how blithely we think of Noah building the ark without appreciating all that it involved for him.

We know that while he was constructing it he preached righteousness to the men of his generation (2 Peter 2:5). Also, if we are right in our assumption, then Noah spent one hundred and twenty years over this project (Genesis 6:3), and Shem, Ham and Japheth were not even born when he began the work. The flood occurred in the six hundredth year of his life and Noah begat them when he was five hundred years old (see Genesis 5:32).

From these facts we can draw certain conclusions.

Firstly, when Noah began to build the ark he did not know that only he and his family would be saved from the flood. It was only when the work was completed that God told him, "For thee have I seen righteous before me in this generation" (Genesis 7:1).

Secondly, during all this time Noah was living a normal family life. In this respect he was no different from us. He had a house to maintain, a living to earn, a family to raise.

Yet at the same time he was engaged in this tremendous building project. When we consider the size of the ark (it was about a hundred yards long and three stories high), we do well to ask ourselves how he coped with such a task. We suggest that he did not do it alone, but that at the beginning he was assisted by the ecclesia of his day.

We might ask, 'What ecclesia?' Consider the genealogy of Genesis 5. It describes the godly line that developed in the earth from Seth.

Of Methuselah (Noah's grandfather, who died in the year of the flood) it is written that "he begat sons and daughters" (Genesis 5:26). His father was Enoch, one of the heroes of faith described for us in Hebrews 11. To his son, Methuselah, he gave a significant name. It means 'He dies and it is sent' (*Fausset's Bible Dictionary*). He was a man of sign. His is the longest recorded life in scripture (969 years) as "the longsuffering of God waited in the days of Noah" (1 Peter 3:20).

Of Lamech, Noah's father, it is also recorded that "he begat sons and daughters" (Genesis 5:30). His declaration concerning Noah at his birth indicates that he was a man who was a true worshipper of the living God (Genesis 5:29).

The picture that emerges therefore is that Noah was a man with uncles and aunts, cousins, brothers and sisters, nephews and nieces, all of them born into the godly line of Seth. They were the ecclesia of Noah's day and from them, we suggest, came the workforce that assisted him in the building of the ark when the task was first begun.

What happened to them? Well, those who remained alive and there must have been many of them, perished in the flood. It is a dreadful thought and a terrible warning to us. When God described to Noah the wickedness of the world in which he lived, He said "that every imagination of the thought of (man's) heart was only evil continually" (Genesis 6:5), and "the earth was filled with violence" (verse 11) – violence such as that demonstrated by Lamech's song of the sword (4:23,24).

69

Strangely, when the Lord Jesus spoke of Noah's days and likened them to the days of his coming, he did not highlight these things. He said:

"They were eating and drinking, marrying and giving in marriage until the day that Noah entered into the ark and knew not until the flood came and took them all away." (Matthew 24:38,39)

In other words, there was a preoccupation with material things to the exclusion of God. Their hearts had been captured by the things that then were to the detriment of the abiding things that related to the Divine purpose.

Now the world has always been concerned with the 'here and now'. It has always been obsessed with material things. Is therefore the Lord speaking, not of the extreme wickedness of the world before the flood, but of the ecclesia of that day? Perhaps they looked at the values and depravity of their age and said, almost in despair, "What is the world coming to?" Yet at the same time, while not involved in debauched wickedness they had given themselves over to a life of self-indulgence. They had filled their lives with material things, unaware of the manner in which they were neglecting to value those abiding things that belonged to the future. They had forgotten that here they had no continuing city.

A final thought about Noah: he was five hundred years old when he begat Shem, Ham and Japheth. This is much older than the age of the other patriarchs when they begat their firstborn. Is it possible that Noah had other children who like their relatives allowed the influences of the world to infiltrate into their lives? If so, we can perhaps relate to Noah when we are saddened that members of our families do not embrace the Truth.

It would also be appropriate that those members of his family that were saved with him in the ark constituted a new generation, a new creation.

By faith Abraham, Isaac and Jacob ...

A mistake sometimes made is to consider Abraham to have been some kind of nomad. In fact, when the God of glory first appeared to him, he lived in Ur of the Chaldees. It was a sophisticated city, a place of culture and learning, and this was the background from which God called him "to go out unto a place which he should after receive for an inheritance ... He went out, not knowing whither he went. By faith he sojourned in the land of promise, as in a strange country, dwelling in tabernacles with Isaac and Jacob, the heirs with him of the same promise: for he looked for a city which hath foundations, whose builder and maker is God" (Hebrews 11:8-10).

Thus the faith of these patriarchs was demonstrated by the fact that they lived in tents. A tent, of course, has no foundations, and it speaks eloquently of the fact that they were, all of them, men with no roots in the world that then was. They were sojourners, that is *temporary* dwellers, in the midst of the land that they had been promised for an *eternal* inheritance. The Greek word indicates "a lodging, to stay as a guest, a temporary abode, lit. dwellers beside" (*Cambridge Bible*).

Those city dwellers amongst whom they lived must have thought their style of living strange. They had no affinity, nothing in common with those amongst whom they dwelt. They looked not at the things that were then, but for the city with a foundation of which God was both the architect and the builder.

The Genesis record is the basis for the words of Hebrews. How easily one misses the emphasis upon the fact that they dwelt in tents (see Genesis 12:8; 13:18; 24:67; 26:17; 31:25; 33:18). Yet of Jacob we are plainly told, "that he was a perfect man, *dwelling in tents*" (Genesis 25:27, RV margin): not perfect in the absolute sense, but an upright man, a man of integrity and the mark of his perfection was the fact that he lived in a tent.

71

"These all died in faith, not having received the promises but having seen them afar off ... (they) confessed that they were strangers and pilgrims on the earth" (Hebrews 11:13). The English word 'pilgrim' conveys the idea of a man who is on a journey; a man who has before him a specific destination. This aspect does not appear to be present in the Greek word used in Hebrews, but the emphasis is upon a lodging place, a temporary resident. However, the word translated 'pilgrim' most certainly suggests 'a traveller' and as such it is appropriate to apply the significance of the English word.

They "looked for a city that had foundations". Thus they had no unnecessary association with the order of things that then was. They were strangers among them; aliens or foreigners, for there they had no continuing city, but sought one to come (13:14).

By faith Moses ...

It is perhaps Moses, most of all, who impresses us with the choice he made between the things that then were and those things that are abiding for which, in faith, he longed.

We can appreciate how Moses would have been instructed by his mother during the time she had with him as a child. She must have been a remarkable woman, for Moses grew up with a sense of destiny – a conviction that it was through him that God would deliver His people from their bondage in Egypt. In the Acts of the Apostles (7:22,23) Stephen tells us that it was when he was full forty years of age that it came into his heart to visit his people. He was not a callow youth, presumptuous in his enthusiasm, but a mature, grown man. He was an intellectual, an eloquent man, a man who had proved himself by the victories that he had won in battle (if Josephus is to be believed). He was a prince of the royal house of Egypt, one of the greatest powers on earth. We might well say that the world lay at his feet: a glittering treasure to be grasped by this powerful man. If he had pursued that career then, no doubt, he would have been buried in the Valley of the Kings. He might have had his own pyramid and perhaps, like Tutankhamen, we could have gone to one of the great museums of the world and seen his sarcophagus and all the riches with which he was buried. People might have stood in wonder and awe at the splendour and magnificence of it all.

But what should really fill us with wonder is the fact that so much human wisdom and ingenuity could be poured into such folly. If he had chosen this course, Moses would now be forgotten before God. He would have no future, for he would have chosen the things that then were to the detriment of the eternal things to which, by God's grace, he had become related.

So Moses visited his people. We must not think of this in terms of our modern use of the word. The scriptural background of the word illuminates the sense of what Moses did:

"(God) hath visited and redeemed his people."

(Luke 1:68)

"God (hath visited) the Gentiles to take out of them a people for his name." (Acts 15:14)

Moses did not casually visit the people of Israel to see how they were coping, but he actually associated himself with them in their suffering. He went and lived amongst them. Thus he refused to be called the son of Pharaoh's daughter, choosing rather to suffer affliction with the people of God (Hebrews 11:24,25).

This is what Hebrews means when it tells us that he forsook Egypt not fearing the wrath of the king. We can well imagine how his actions would have appeared at the royal court; how the amazement they would experience at first would have turned eventually to fury as Pharaoh himself came to appreciate that this behaviour (in his eyes) was treasonable.

What Moses had not appreciated was that the time was not right for the longed-for deliverance. He needed to learn through forty years of exile in the land of Midian that it was not a prince of the royal house of

Egypt who was to accomplish this deliverance, but a man humbled to appreciate his weakness, and that it was God alone by His power and might who would effect this act of redemption.

We should, however, in no way allow this fact to diminish the remarkable faith that Moses showed in behaving as he did. He "esteemed the reproach of Christ greater riches than the treasures in Egypt: for he had respect unto the recompense of the reward ... He endured as seeing him who is invisible" (verses 26,27).

Thus Moses saw the transient and fleeting nature of the things that then were. For he turned his back on this world and everything it had to offer. "He looked to the reward" (RSV). He allowed nothing to distract him as with a fixed gaze he looked to that city that has foundations, whose builder and maker is God. He endured as seeing Him who is invisible. What a tremendous paradox! It speaks to us of his God-consciousness; his awareness of the reality of God: his spiritual discernment in those things that related to the Divine purpose. In this respect, nothing has changed and Moses remains an eloquent testimony to us of the importance of having a true perception of the fact that here we have no continuing city.

The Lord Jesus Christ

The supreme example of faith is the Lord Jesus himself. It is in him that all God's promises of His coming kingdom are yea and amen (2 Corinthians 1:20). It is the resurrection of the Lord Jesus that has made all these things sure. It is his victory that should assure us of the certainty that God will establish the city that has foundations.

The world in which we live is ever changing. The material things it has to offer might seem sometimes to be attractive and offer us lasting satisfaction and happiness. Sometimes it is a hard lesson to learn that all these things are transient and fleeting and can give no lasting fulfilment. Like Moses we have to develop a fixed gaze that can see beyond the things that are now, to those things that are eternal. The exhortation of Hebrews is, "Looking unto Jesus the author and finisher of our faith" (12:2).

In the midst of all life's changing scenes we have to turn our backs on the things that now are, and look to him who is "the same yesterday, to day and for ever". In all life's vicissitudes he abides changeless, and offers to us the promise of an eternal inheritance.

Like those heroes of faith described in Hebrews, we must learn the true value of the things that are now, compared with the abiding things that belong to God's kingdom, "for here we have no continuing city, but we seek one to come".

15

TWO TEMPTATIONS

THERE are two notable accounts of temptations in the pages of scripture. First of all, there is the account of the temptation of our first parents by the serpent (Genesis 3). Secondly there is the temptation of the Lord Jesus Christ in the wilderness, recorded in Matthew 4 and Luke 4.

Adam and Eve

When the Lord God created man in His image it was His intention that Adam, possessing the ability to relate to Him and worship Him, should develop his personality in the likeness of the divine character. We do not always appreciate, however, that physically Adam and Eve were created as mature adult beings, yet at the moment of creation they were characterless. Unlike us they had no childhood, no teenage years or early adult life. Consequently they did not have the opportunity to develop character and to be moulded by the vicissitudes of life that we experience.

How then was character to be developed? We can be sure that encompassed in the words "very good", that were used to describe the man and the woman, was an exceptional intellect that would have made them of "quick understanding" in things relating to the Lord God. And if we are not mistaken they would have been taught by angelic ministration and very quickly have learned those things that it was necessary for them to know. Character, however, is not formed by knowledge alone. To know what is right is only the first step and the understanding of what God requires must be put into practice. It is through experience that character is formed. It is necessary that the individual is tested by the circumstances of life. Thus it was that God gave one prohibition:

"Of every tree of the garden thou mayest freely eat: but of the tree of the knowledge of good and evil, thou shalt not eat of it: for in the day that thou eatest thereof thou shalt surely die."   (Genesis 2:16,17)

The temptation

Was this one commandment sufficient to produce the character that God desired them to have? The answer is that in conjunction with the environment in which they lived and their experience of the goodness of God it was. Consider first how everything God had created and provided for them spoke of His love. In the creation of Eve He had recognised Adam's need for a suitable companion with whom he could find happiness and fulfilment. In addition to the instruction they would have received, they were surrounded in that garden by all the tokens of God's concern for their well-being. Consequently, they should have developed a conviction that the prohibition regarding the tree of the knowledge of good and evil could only be for their benefit.

The serpent, however, in his subtlety suggested that this was not the case. In effect he claimed that God had deprived them of the best; they would not die but would become like the angels with whom they had association in the garden. He slandered God (N.B. the origin of the devil). It was as though he said, 'You don't need to do it God's way, there is an easier way; you can take a short cut to obtain all the satisfaction and fulfilment that your heart desires'.

Faced by this test of their fidelity they could have demonstrated their love for God, their understanding of His character and all that He had done for them. By believing His word they would have shown faith. In the persistence of the serpent they would have had opportunity to show endurance and longsuffering, and in their hearts they would have experienced a deeper joy and peace in the fullness of the fellowship they enjoyed with their Creator. Thus from that one

77

command could have developed all the attributes of character in which the Lord God delighted.

Fundamentally, all sin is an act of slander against God; it is a rejection of His word. If we might sum it up briefly, God has said, "This is the way, walk ye in it", and if we recognise the love and concern that He has for humankind we shall acknowledge also that His way is the only means whereby it is possible to obtain lasting happiness and satisfaction. The thinking of the serpent, however (the devil within), convinces us that our own way is better. We reject God's word and seek to find fulfilment and satisfaction by following our own inclinations. Thus, in effect, we slander God, treating His word as though it were not true.

How significant it is therefore that God should esteem faith in His word as essential to forgiveness – in short, we are justified by faith (see Genesis 15:6).

"Thou art my beloved Son"

It is evident from both Matthew and Luke that the Lord's wilderness temptation arose directly out of his baptism and the declaration made by the voice from heaven: "This is my beloved Son, in whom I am well pleased" (Matthew 3:17). There can be little doubt that the reference is to Psalm 2 – a song that speaks in eloquent tones of the day of Messiah's glory:

"Yet have I set my king upon my holy hill of Zion. I will declare the decree: the LORD hath said unto me, Thou art my Son; this day have I begotten thee. Ask of me, and I shall give thee the heathen for thine inheritance, and the uttermost parts of the earth for thy possession." (verses 6-8)

It spoke to him unquestionably about the fact that one day he would sit upon the throne of his father David forever. Notice, however, that into the reference from the psalm is inserted the word "beloved". The significance of this word would not have been lost upon the Lord Jesus. It is in fact a one word quotation from the Old Testament. In Genesis 22 the expression "thine only son" is to be found three times (verses 2,12,16). Of the word 'only' used in this instance (and almost always of an only child in the rest of the Old Testament), *Strong's Concordance* tells us that by implication it means 'beloved': thus, "take now thy beloved Son". The Lord Jesus would have been reminded of Abraham's willingness to offer his beloved son and from the depth of his understanding of scripture he would also have appreciated that for him there could be no divine intervention. In the purpose of God, He would not spare His own Son, but would deliver him up for us all (Romans 8:32).

So by linking the words of Psalm 2 and Genesis 22 in this remarkable fashion the voice from heaven spoke to the Lord of the two aspects of his work, for before the crown there must be the cross.

"In whom my soul delighteth"

To these two Old Testament allusions the voice from heaven added a third:

> "Behold my servant, whom I uphold; mine elect, in whom my soul delighteth; I have put my spirit upon him: he shall bring forth judgment to the Gentiles."
>
> (Isaiah 42:1)

"In whom I am well pleased" expresses the meaning of the Hebrew words of the prophet Isaiah precisely. Here was encouragement for the Lord Jesus: a reminder of the great work that had been committed to his trust and an expression of his Father's delight in the manner in which he had conducted himself up to this time.

Again the voice from heaven spoke to him of the path he must tread. He had not just come for Israel but his work was to embrace the Gentiles also. Knowing the scriptures as no other man, the Lord would have grasped the context which spoke of his being given –

> "for a covenant of the people, for a light of the Gentiles; to open the blind eyes, to bring out the prisoners from the prison, and them that sit in darkness out of the prison house." (verses 6,7)

79

Implicit in the concept of a covenant is the principle of sacrifice. So once more the Lord Jesus would have been reminded of the purpose of his coming. To fulfil the will of God he must go on that path of self-sacrifice and self-denial that would bring him finally to the cross. The result of his work was that the blindness of Israel and the darkness of the Gentiles would be lifted and both would be delivered from the prison house.

Thus the voice from heaven spoke of the great issues that confronted him as he commenced his ministry, and it was this matter of the cross before the crown that was at the heart of his temptation in the wilderness. In effect the devil said to him, as the serpent said to Eve, 'There is a short cut to the kingdom – you can avoid the cross – why don't you take it?'

"Man shall not live by bread alone"

The temptation came to him:

"If thou be the Son of God, command that these stones be made bread." (Matthew 4:3)

If it were purely a question of satisfying his own hunger the matter could easily have been resolved without resorting to miracle. He could have returned to the nearest town or village and satisfied his hunger there. But there was much more to the temptation than that. His hunger was the trigger that caused him to reflect on the suffering and deprivation of the poor in Israel and indeed in the world at large. Implicit in the words "Son of God" was the promise of the throne. He would have been reminded of the day for which Israel looked when Messiah should satisfy the poor of Zion with bread (Psalm 132:15), when there should be an abundance of corn in the top of the mountains and the fruit would shake like Lebanon (72:16). Why then should he not use his power to satisfy the needs of the hungry, to fill the stomachs of the poor of this world? In essence the question was, Why not avoid the cross and bestow the blessings of the kingdom now?

The Lord's response came directly from the word of God. He honoured God's word whereas Adam and Eve denied it: "It is written, Man shall not live by bread alone, but by every word that proceedeth out of the mouth of God" (Matthew 4:4, quoting Deuteronomy 8:3).

To have embarked on a ministry of social reform, feeding the hungry, seeking to solve the problems of poverty and injustice would have been a negation of the will of God. In the compassion he showed, in the miracles he performed, limited in their impact on the world at large, the Lord Jesus demonstrated that one day he would resolve all the problems that confronted mankind. But first he must go the way of the cross, for unless he did so men would still die; sin would still reign and man's inhumanity to his fellow man would still blight the earth. Only by embracing the living word of God could men and women become related to those eternal things that were offered in the Gospel and know the joy of the kingdom age.

There is an exhortation here for us. While showing compassion for the suffering of our fellows and doing what we can to give comfort and to alleviate their pain and adversity, this is not the primary responsibility committed to our trust. Our first duty is to preach the word that men might have hope of eternal life. How careful we must be of involvement in the world's organisations that seek to reform that which they perceive to be wrong with this present order of things and to put right all the social injustice and inequality that exists. Man does not live by bread alone but by every word that proceeds out of the mouth of God.

"Thou shalt not tempt the Lord thy God"

Taken up to the pinnacle of the temple the Lord Jesus was reminded of the words of Psalm 91:

> "He shall give his angels charge concerning thee: and in their hands they shall bear thee up, lest at any time thou dash thy foot against a stone."
>
> (verses 11,12; cited Matthew 4:6)

His response was taken once more from the book of Deuteronomy:

81

"It is written again, Thou shalt not tempt the Lord thy God." (6:16; quoted Matthew 4:7)

It might be thought that the point of this temptation was to give the people one tremendous public sign that would convince them that this man was unquestionably the promised Messiah. However, the works that the Lord Jesus performed during his ministry were in themselves sufficient proof of his identity, yet they still crucified him.

At the heart of the temptation is still the question of the cross. The context in Deuteronomy holds the key: "Ye shall not tempt the LORD your God, as ye tempted him in Massah". The record of events at Massah is to be found in Exodus 17 (verses 1-7). Here Israel complained because there was no water to drink and "tempted the LORD, saying, Is the LORD among us, or not?" The tempting lay in the fact that they tried to put God to the proof. They did not trust His word but asked for a visible assurance that He did not intend to destroy them.

So also the subtlety of the Lord's temptation lay in the underlying thought: 'How can you be certain that when you lie still and unknowing in the coldness of the grave He will raise you up again? Well, why not put Him to the test? Cast yourself down from the pinnacle and see if His angels really will bear you up'. Once more it is the fidelity of God's word that is called in question and the Lord Jesus triumphed gloriously in demonstrating his unshakable trust in what was written.

This trust was demonstrated on the cross when the Lord uttered his last words with a quotation from scripture: "Father, into thy hands I commend my spirit" (Luke 23:46, citing Psalm 31:5). He committed himself to his Father and the next words of the psalm describe his next conscious moment: "Thou hast redeemed me, O LORD God of truth". God's word proved faithful in the performance, at the appropriate time, of what had been spoken.

82

"Thou shalt worship the Lord thy God"

From "an exceeding high mountain" the Lord Jesus was shown all the kingdoms of the world, together with their glory, and told that all these could be his if only he would fall down and worship the devil (Matthew 4:8,9). Of course, the voice from heaven had confirmed his Sonship in the words of Psalm 2, and the same passage had declared that God would give him the nations for his inheritance and the uttermost parts of the earth for his possession (verse 8).

Why then should this temptation present the Lord with any problem at all? Once again the issue was between the cross and the crown. If he had tried to take the kingdom then it would have been an attempt to evade the cross. It would have been a denial of God's word. If he had succeeded in possessing the kingdom then it would not have been God's way and it would not have been His kingdom. The Lord's response was: "Thou shalt worship the Lord thy God, and him only shalt thou serve" (Matthew 4:10) – another quotation from the book of Deuteronomy (6:13). Again the context illuminates the Lord's spiritual insight. When God brought His people into the land, Moses said it would be to give them –

> "great and goodly cities, which thou buildest not, and houses full of all good things, which thou filledst not, and wells digged, which thou diggedst not, vineyards and olive trees, which thou plantedst not; when thou shalt have eaten and be full; then beware lest thou forget the LORD, which brought thee forth out of the land of Egypt, from the house of bondage. Thou shalt fear the LORD thy God, and serve him … "
> (6:10-13)

In a marvellous way the Lord Jesus had captured the significance of the context for it was to be God's kingdom, not man's, and all the glory belonged to Him. The only way it could be established was in the way He had determined and that meant the Lord Jesus treading the path to the cross. As he began his public ministry, this he resolved to do.

In a dramatic way the temptation in the wilderness sums up the moment of decision towards which all his life had led him and points to the recurring nature of the crisis with which he lived throughout his ministry. We see the temptation to turn the stones into bread latent in the feeding of the 5,000 and the 4,000; the Lord said they sought him not because of the miracles but because they ate of the loaves and were filled (John 6:26). The temptation to succumb to their wishes must have been very real. Similarly, after the feeding of the 5,000 they would have taken him by force to make him a king. It needed long hours of prayer alone in the mountain to strengthen his resolve to continue on his chosen path (verse 15). At Nazareth the Jews would have cast him headlong from the top of the hill – a wonderful opportunity to have put the words of Psalm 91 to the proof, but the Lord "passing through the midst of them went his way" (Luke 4:28-30).

"As a man chasteneth his son"

Remarkably, with the whole of the Old Testament before him, the Lord Jesus quoted three times from Deuteronomy (chapters 6 and 8). There is a very good reason for this. Not only were the Lord's responses appropriate to the questions posed by the temptations, but it has to be remembered that the voice from heaven had declared him to be the Son of God. Each temptation had questioned the reality of that fact: "If thou be the Son of God ..." So Deuteronomy 8 had affirmed:

> "Thou shalt also consider in thine heart, that, as a man chasteneth his son, so the LORD thy God chasteneth thee." (verse 5)

The chapters spoke of Israel's sonship. They were consequently perfectly suited to the circumstances of the only begotten Son of God; for "though he were a Son, yet learned he obedience by the things which he suffered", and being made like unto his brethren he himself "suffered being tempted".

16

THE DEATH OF STEPHEN

IT is not intended to consider the defence that Stephen offered when he stood before the Council. Rather our concern is to examine the concluding words of his address, the response this evoked in the Jews and the record of his death (Acts 7:48-60). It is sufficient to say regarding his defence of the Gospel that its theme is to show that the God of Israel could not be confined by the borders of the land of Israel, nor His presence limited to a house built by hands in the city of Jerusalem. He was indeed the God of all the earth and consequently the Gospel message must also be for the Gentiles.

The conclusion of his address

When Stephen began to speak we are told that they saw his face "as it had been the face of an angel" (6:15). It is surely significant that Stephen should have concluded his defence by reminding them that they had received the law by the disposition of angels but had not kept it (7:53). Their reaction therefore to his words was in keeping with the manner in which they had rejected that which was ordained by angels (Galatians 3:19). So now they allowed prejudice and rage to blind them to the truth of the message that Stephen delivered. He concluded his speech with some words of the prophet Isaiah:

"Heaven is my throne, and earth is my footstool: what house will ye build me? saith the Lord: or what is the place of my rest? Hath not my hand made all these things?"   (Acts 7:49,50; citing Isaiah 66:1,2)

Of tremendous significance, and undoubtedly the trigger that caused the paroxysm of rage, so that they were cut to the heart and gnashed on him with their teeth, were Stephen's next words when compared with the words of the prophet. Isaiah had said:

> "But to this man will I look, even to him that is poor and of a contrite spirit, and trembleth at my word." (66:2)

The words are familiar to *us*; how much more so to the members of the Council, versed as they were in their Old Testament scriptures. We can imagine as Stephen began to quote this well known passage how their minds would have run ahead and anticipated the familiar words. Stephen, however, did not quote them. Instead he uttered an indictment that was the complete antithesis of everything that those beautiful words of the prophet conveyed:

> "Ye stiffnecked and uncircumcised in heart and ears, ye do always resist the Holy Spirit: as your fathers did, so do ye. Which of the prophets have not your fathers persecuted? And they have slain them which shewed before of the coming of the Just One; of whom ye have been now the betrayers and murderers." (Acts 7:51,52)

Could any words have been more telling? Understanding immediately the significance of Stephen's charge against them, the frenzy of their anger overwhelmed all sense of guilt they might have felt.

"Looking stedfastly into heaven"

The record in Acts tells us that at this moment, when their fury against him was at its fiercest, Stephen gazing intently into heaven saw the glory of God and the Lord Jesus standing at His right hand. In his own words:

> "Behold, I see the heavens opened, and the Son of man standing on the right hand of God." (verse 56)

Interestingly, the same Greek word translated "stedfastly", to describe the manner in which Stephen looked into heaven, was used of the way in which the

Council beheld Stephen when they saw his face "as it had been the face of an angel". It helps us to appreciate the different ways in which their minds were focused. They, having accepted the evidence of false witnesses, were intent only on convicting him. That they saw his face as that of an angel is surely a testimony to the serenity of spirit he displayed and the confidence with which he stood before them.

At that moment when their anger erupted Stephen showed no fear, for his mind was full of the second coming of his Lord and the glory that should follow. To sustain him in that hope God graciously granted him a vision of that glory with the Lord Jesus standing on the right hand of God.

The Lord Jesus standing

It has been said that the Lord was standing as a mark of respect and acknowledgement of the sacrifice that this faithful witness made; it was an assurance that the Lord was with him and that his eternal future was secure. All this is surely true but possibly we can see a little more, for what would this vision have conveyed to the mind of Stephen? He was a man who like the members of the Council had an extensive knowledge of the Old Testament scriptures, and more than them a remarkable insight into the meaning of what was written.

He describes the Lord Jesus as "the Son of man". This is a title used in the Gospel records exclusively by the Lord Jesus, concerning himself. One instance, in particular, seems to have a direct reference to Stephen's experience. In response to the question of the high priest, the Lord said:

"Hereafter shall ye see the Son of man sitting on the right hand of power, and coming in the clouds of heaven."   (Matthew 26:64)

The words of the Lord Jesus bring together two passages of Old Testament scripture: Daniel 7:13,14 and Psalm 110:1. The passage in Daniel speaks of what we might describe as the investiture of "the Son of man"

87

(surely the multitudinous body of the redeemed). When brought with the clouds of heaven before the Ancient of days there is given him "dominion, and glory, and a kingdom, that all people, nations, and languages, should serve him".

The passage from the Psalms describes David's Lord as sitting at God's right hand until that time came when his enemies should be made his footstool. Thus the Lord affirmed before the high priest that he would be exalted to his Father's right hand until that time came when he would come with the clouds of heaven and establish God's kingdom, all opposition falling before him. Stephen's declaration of that which he saw clearly revolves around these scriptures.

There is, of course, the important distinction that he saw the Lord *standing*. What would this have conveyed to the mind of such a man, mighty in the word of God? No longer *sitting* but *standing*: therefore the time had come when the Lord should descend to take his kingdom and reign; the time when he should come again with the clouds of heaven. But this time, of course, had not yet come. What then did he see? Surely a vision of the future – a revelation that spoke to him of that day on which his heart was set. This understanding of what Stephen saw is perhaps reinforced by the fact that he saw "the heavens opened".

Is it possible that another Old Testament scripture lies behind these words?

"Oh that thou wouldest rend the heavens, that thou wouldest come down, that the mountains might flow down at thy presence." (Isaiah 64:1)

The background to Isaiah's words is to be found in the record of God's manifestation of Himself to Israel at Sinai (see Exodus 19:18-20). Then God came down and revealed His law to Moses. Isaiah's prayer is that once more God would come down as at Sinai. So also Stephen longed with all his heart for that day when "the Lord himself shall descend from heaven with a shout, with the voice of the archangel, and with the trump of God:

and the dead in Christ shall rise first" (1 Thessalonians 4:16; note the echoes of Exodus 19).

It is surely significant that Isaiah 64 contains the words later quoted by the Apostle Paul:

"For since the beginning of the world men have not heard, nor perceived by the ear, neither hath the eye seen, O God, beside thee, what he hath prepared for him that waiteth for him."

(verse 4; cp. 1 Corinthians 2:9)

So Stephen could face death, his mind totally focused on the coming of his Lord and the things that God has prepared for those that love Him. What a remarkable thing it is, if we accept that it was a vision of the future, that in his last moments of life Stephen saw the Lord standing ready to descend and in his next conscious moment the Lord will have come.

Stephen's death

The manner of his death bears many similarities to the death of the Lord Jesus. As the Lord was crucified "without the camp" (Hebrews 13:13) so also they "cast him out of the city, and stoned him" (Acts 7:58). The prayer of the Lord Jesus for those who crucified him was, "Father forgive them; for they know not what they do" (Luke 23:34). Likewise Stephen prayed for those responsible for his death, beseeching the Lord that this sin might not be laid to their charge.

A principle emerges here of which we need to take account. We know that forgiveness of sin is dependent on repentance; that there must first be an acknowledgement and confession of sin. Were therefore the words of the Lord Jesus and those of Stephen a request that these sins should be forgiven without the usual conditions being observed? Surely not! It was first a recognition that, on both of these occasions, God's anger would have been aroused against those who had perpetrated these evil deeds. Yet in the hearts of the Lord Jesus and of Stephen, his faithful witness, there was no desire for revenge. Rather there was a plea that if they sought forgiveness it might be freely given.

As they stoned Stephen he called upon the Lord Jesus to receive his spirit (verse 59) and the words he used are, of course, reminiscent of the last words spoken by the Lord on the cross:

"Father, into thy hands I commend my spirit."

(Luke 23:46)

This is a quotation from Psalm 31:5 and significantly the next words of the psalm record his next conscious moment:

"Thou hast redeemed me, O LORD God of truth."

How appropriate then that Stephen should have echoed the words of his Lord as in vision he saw him ready to descend, for in his next waking moment the Lord will have come.

It has been said that the words of Psalm 31 were taught by the Jews to their children: it was their prayer before they went to sleep each night and their acknowledgement that God had kept them through the hours of darkness to the dawn of a new day. How poignant then is the record of the death of this faithful man: "he fell asleep" (Acts 7:60).

A crown of glory

The name Stephen means a 'crown' – not the diadem but the coronal wreath of victory that was given to the victor in the games. This crown was bestowed as a mark of honour and respect in recognition of some public service. Usually of laurel leaves wound together, it would soon fade away and the honour associated with it would be forgotten.

How wonderful then to contemplate the beautiful words of promise written by the Apostle Peter that there is laid up for all God's faithful servants "a crown of glory that fadeth not away" (1 Peter 5:4).

17

"TAKE HEED"

FOUR times in Mark 13 the Lord Jesus Christ exhorted his disciples to "take heed". The Greek word *blepo* means literally 'to look at', and a consideration of the contexts in which the Lord used these words shows that he was emphasising the importance of not only looking at external events, but also the need to look at ourselves to ensure that we are being vigilant and alert to maintain our faithfulness in the midst of life's changing circumstances.

False Christs

In response to the question that the disciples asked about the destruction of the temple (verse 4), the Lord Jesus said:

"Take heed lest any man deceive you: for many shall come in my name, saying, I am Christ; and shall deceive many." (verses 5,6)

The word translated "deceive" means literally 'to cause to roam, or to wander away'. Notice that the false teachers shall "come in my name". In other words, although undoubtedly there were many false Christs who rose up in the days prior to the destruction of Jerusalem, the greatest danger to believers was from within their own ranks. The uncertainties of the times, wars, rumours of wars, earthquakes and famines (verses 7,8) would give men ample scope to suggest that the Lord's coming was imminent and to influence them with teaching that was contrary to "the faith which was once for all delivered unto the saints" (Jude verse 3, RV).

What lessons can we draw from these first century circumstances? Well for them, only thirty or so years had passed since the Lord's ascension into heaven. For us, nearly two thousand years have gone by and still the Lord has not come. Our danger is that men will say, "Where is the promise of his coming?" (2 Peter 3:4). So many times world events have created a sense of expectancy and urgency only to settle down again, that we hear discordant voices claiming to speak in his name, seeking to bring us to think more of the immanence of Christ (i.e., his presence with us now) than of the imminence of his return. These are two very similar looking and sounding words but the one puts the emphasis on the present, and the other on the future. We must not underestimate the work of the Lord Jesus Christ in our lives now; he does truly dwell with us (John 14:23). But our spiritual experiences now are not an end in themselves, for they prepare us for the future – for the day of our Lord's coming. It is to that day we must look. Wherefore let us take heed, for "surely I come quickly ... Even so, come, Lord Jesus" (Revelation 22:20).

Persecution and adversity

"But take heed to yourselves: for they shall deliver you up to councils; and in the synagogues ye shall be beaten: and ye shall be brought before rulers and kings for my sake, for a testimony against them."

(Mark 13:9)

The Lord Jesus never promised that living the Truth would be easy. Every age brings its own problems and although we do not have to face the intensity of persecution experienced by the early believers, we too, if we are faithful to our calling, can be reviled of men. However, if there is not the persecution of earlier days, the difficulties we face must never be underestimated. We must "take heed to ourselves".

In Numbers 21 we read how Israel were "much discouraged because of the way" and their soul loathed the light bread (verses 4,5). In other words, they could not face the hardship any longer and they despised the manna which God had provided to chasten and instruct them. The result was that "much people of Israel died" (verse 6). The point to note, however, is that when Israel became discouraged (AV margin, "shortened") in this way, there were only seven months remaining before they entered the land (see Numbers 20:26 and 33:38). They were almost there when their lack of staying power finally manifested itself. Faced by the difficulties and trials of our pilgrimage, we have to ask ourselves whether we have the ability to hold fast to the hope we have embraced. What a disaster it would be if, at the very portals of the kingdom of God, with the coming of the Lord imminent, we were to let slide the eternal treasures committed to our trust, for "he that shall endure *unto the end*, the same shall be saved" (Mark 13:13).

The comfort of prophecy

"But take ye heed: behold, I have foretold you all things" (verse 23). This chapter, of course, contains the 'Olivet Prophecy' and foretells the events associated with the destruction of Jerusalem in AD 68-70. It also speaks of the events that will precede the coming of the Lord. The fact that God has spoken in this way, foretelling the course of world history in relation to the outworking of His purpose, should be a source of great comfort and consolation to us. The message is that God rules in the kingdom of men. That means that history is not purposeless and meaningless but it is all leading somewhere. God is guiding events until eventually, at the coming of the Lord and the establishing of the kingdom, God's purpose will be consummated in the earth. Because of this we need not be afraid, however dreadful world events might appear. Although men's hearts might fail them for fear because of the things that are coming upon the earth, if our gaze is fixed firmly on the coming of the Lord, if we are taking heed to ourselves and our own attitude to spiritual things, then we shall know a peace and confidence in our hearts that none of this world's troubles can snatch away from us.

"Watch ye therefore"

The final part of this chapter (verses 24-37) deals with the events surrounding the Lord's manifestation in the earth and offers us the opportunity to reiterate the points of exhortation already made. The parable of the fig tree (verse 28) is a powerful reminder to us of the work of God in regathering His people. The State of Israel is a constant witness that the day is near: "When ye shall see these things come to pass, know that it is nigh, even at the door" (verse 29).

The Lord reminds us: "Of that day and that hour knoweth no man" (verse 32). That is not a reason for slothfulness and apathy but an exhortation to vigilance and watchfulness, for, "Take ye heed, watch and pray: for ye know not when the time is" (verse 33).

Let us never underestimate the power of prayer in this situation, for watching and praying go together. By our prayers we show how great is our longing and desire for God's kingdom to come. Watching the signs of the times, together with our own heart and conduct in the midst of this wicked generation, will ensure that when the Lord comes he will not find us sleeping (verse 36). This is not referring to literal sleep of course, but spiritual lethargy and apathy: allowing ourselves to be overcome by the cares and anxieties of this life; allowing the material things of life to fill our hearts so that they appear to be all that really matters. This is the opiate the world offers to lull us into a sense of false security, to drug us so that we are insensitive to the word of God and its message. In this way the world can overwhelm us and we can let slip the things that belong to God's kingdom and glory.

Mark 13 is a wonderful chapter. It holds out a glorious vision of God's future work in the earth. To believers of all ages it gives salutary words of warning and advice, for the Lord Jesus said to his disciples:

"What I say unto you I say unto all, Watch."

(verse 37)

18

"THOU SHALT SEE GREATER ABOMINATIONS"

THE eighth chapter of Ezekiel tells how the prophet was carried by the spirit, from the land of his captivity, back to Jerusalem to behold and witness against the abominations that were defiling the house of God (verses 1-3).

There at the door of the inner gate that looked towards the north, the place where the brazen altar was situated, this rebellious people had erected an image to a strange god. It is described as an "image of jealousy, which provoketh to jealousy" (verses 3 and 5). The description carries us back in thought to the words of Deuteronomy 32: "They provoked him to jealousy with strange gods, with abominations provoked they him to anger" (verse 16).

"No man can serve two masters"

God will not share the honour that is due to Him with any other and when men seek to give to false gods that which belongs to Him alone, then He is provoked to jealousy. The sheer effrontery of men who could erect an image to a false god in the very portals of the house of God leaves us almost breathless in amazement. Yet what of us who are "living stones" in the spiritual house that God is building? Do we, for instance, try to serve God and mammon? Have we got divided hearts? Have we erected in our lives false gods on which we spend our money, our time and energy? It remains true for us as for Israel of old that God will not share our hearts or our allegiance. If we have erected and worshipped the "gods of this world" in our lives, then like Israel we provoke the Lord "to jealousy".

The matter, however, did not rest there, for God said to Ezekiel:

> "Seest thou what they do? Even the great abominations that the house of Israel committeth here, that I should go far off from my sanctuary? But turn thee yet again, and thou shalt see greater abominations." (verse 6)

So the prophet was brought to the door of the court and when he looked he saw a hole in the wall. He was commanded to dig in the wall and there he saw a door (verses 7,8):

> "And he said unto me, Go in, and behold the wicked abominations that they do here." (verse 9)

There he saw –

> "every form of creeping things, and abominable beasts, and all the idols of the house of Israel, portrayed upon the wall round about." (verse 10)

God asked him:

> "Hast thou seen what the ancients of the house of Israel do in the dark, every man in the chambers of his imagery? For they say, The LORD seeth us not." (verse 12)

The deceitfulness of sin

In the midst of these abominations there were seventy men of the ancients of the house of Israel, the ruling council of the people – those who should have given spiritual guidance, but who instead were totally implicated in the sin of the people. In the midst of them stood Jaazaniah, the son of Shaphan (verse 11). His name means "Yahweh is listening" and yet they said, "The LORD seeth us not", and it was with deep irony that God told them that when His judgements were among them because of their wickedness, then "though they cry in mine ear with a loud voice, yet will I not hear them" (verse 18).

Again we pause to reflect, for what have we hidden in our hearts? What do we do in the dark? Have we too got chambers of imagery? We must remember that God does not need to dig through the wall to open the door to our hearts, for He knows what is there. We may have arrayed ourselves with many layers of disguise to deceive our brethren and sisters, but we cannot deceive Him.

Perhaps there is a simple test that we can apply to ourselves. Would we be ashamed if everybody knew what we did in secret – if the hidden things of our hearts, the things we do in the dark, were dragged out into the full light of day? Would our brethren and sisters recognise us? Would those who thought they knew us best say, "Is that really you, the brother or sister I thought I knew so well?"

Again, however, the matter did not rest there. Twice more (verses 13,15) the prophet is told, "Thou shalt see greater abominations than these"; the people sank deeper and deeper into the mire of their iniquity. It is an appalling picture but again a powerful exhortation, for what a commentary it provides upon human nature and the deceitfulness of sin. The first sin is usually the most difficult to commit; the second is easier and the more we indulge in wrongdoing the simpler it becomes. We become hardened to it; sin deceives us and eventually we are unaware that we are sinning at all. This can be true of a particular course of action in our lives. But having reached that point, the danger is we shall go beyond it and pursue another course of action that will take us even deeper into the mire. The truth is there are no depths to which human nature will not sink, and how many are there who, viewing the ruin they have made of their lives, can only wonder that things they once rejected and abhorred have now become a part of their everyday lives.

"Take heed"

We have painted a sombre picture but we must not leave it there. We have used this chapter to depict the depths to which human nature can sink and the dangers to which we are all exposed. If we have not trodden the downward spiral that the chapter depicts

97

then let us take heed lest we fall, and learn from the mistakes of Israel of old. If we have begun that journey and recognise ourselves in the modern forms of that ancient apostasy, then like the Psalmist, let us enter the sanctuary, meditate and learn the awful consequences of pursuing this way of life:

"But as for me, my feet were almost gone; my steps had well nigh slipped. For I was envious at the foolish … They are not in trouble as other men … And they say, How doth God know? And is there knowledge in the most High? Behold, these are the ungodly, who prosper in the world; they increase in riches. Verily I have cleansed my heart in vain, and washed my hands in innocency … When I thought to know this, it was too painful for me; until I went into the sanctuary of God: then understood I their end. Surely thou didst set them in slippery places …"

(Psalm 73:2-5,11-19)

And if, sadly, there are any that have plumbed the very depths of spiritual depravity, then recognise the sin into which the waywardness of our nature has led us; acknowledge and confess it before God in the sure knowledge that –

"If we confess our sins, he is faithful and just to forgive us our sins, and to cleanse us from all unrighteousness." (1 John 1:9)

The Apostle Paul wrote, "But where sin abounded, grace did much more abound" (Romans 5:20). Sin is like a weed or a canker; when once it has taken root it establishes itself, it spreads. There is a power in it that enables it to abound so that it can reign as a king in a man's life.

But where sin abounds, grace much more abounds (literally, "it super-abounds"). The idea is of the piling on of more and yet more grace until the power of sin is finally eclipsed. Sin is strong but grace is stronger. If only we turn to God in that humble and contrite spirit that recognises our sin, pleading for God's forgiveness, then we can rejoice with the apostle in the knowledge:

"that as sin hath reigned unto death, even so might grace reign through righteousness unto eternal life by Jesus Christ our Lord." (Romans 5:21)

19

ALONE IN PRAYER

IN John chapter 6 we have the record of the Feeding of the Five Thousand. Following this miracle the excitement and enthusiasm of the people was such that they would have taken the Lord Jesus by force and made him a king.

Faced by this crisis he sent his disciples to the other side of the lake, whereas he departed into a mountain alone to find strength and help from his Father in prayer. It was there, on the mountain tops and in solitary places, alone with God, and separated from all the distractions of his busy life, that the Lord Jesus communed with his Father. This, of course, was the customary way in which he found strength and sought guidance to face the great issues that confronted him in his ministry (see also Mark 1:35 and Luke 6:12).

A two-way relationship

When we think of our own personal prayers then, no doubt, we find it difficult to understand how the Lord could sustain his prayer over such a protracted period of time. However, if we think of his experience as primarily an act of communion, that is, a two-way relationship, for he was talking to God and God was talking to him, then it becomes easier for us to understand. It is John's record that helps us to appreciate this perspective.

The Lord Jesus testifies of himself:

"And *what he hath seen and heard*, that he testifieth." (3:32)

"I have many things to say and to judge of you: but he that sent me is true; and I speak to the world *those things that I have heard of him.*" (8:26)

"But now ye seek to kill me, a man that hath told you the truth, *which I have heard of God.*"   (8:40)

"... for all things *that I have heard of my Father* I have made known unto you."   (15:15)

It is a characteristic of John's record and surely it means precisely what it says. These things had been heard audibly by the Lord Jesus when, as with Moses, his Father had spoken to him face to face when he was alone with Him in the solitary places. The Lord was not only talking to God but he was listening and learning.

There is a lesson for us to learn about prayer from the Lord's example. For when we are alone with God, withdrawn from all that would distract, there will be occasions when our prayers will turn, instinctively, to contemplation and meditation upon the word of God. In this way God will speak to us and we shall learn of Him from our reflections on His word.

Jacob at Jabbok

The experiences of the Lord Jesus are reflected in the lives of all faithful men and women and the life of the patriarch Jacob provides us with an excellent illustration.

As he returned from Padan-aram, fearful of the anger of his brother Esau, he was met by the angels of God. He called the place Mahanaim and the margin of the AV tells us that the word means "two hosts, or, camps" (RV margin, "two hosts or companies"). There was the company of Jacob and encircling them, protecting them, there was the camp of the angels (Genesis 32:1,2; see also Psalm 34:7). Clearly this was intended to reassure Jacob and to quell the fear and anxiety that he felt.

It seems, however, that Jacob was not totally convinced by this revelation of angelic protection for when messengers brought him the news that Esau was approaching with four hundred men he was filled with fear and distress and, as a precaution, divided his camp into two companies (Genesis 32:7,8). This does not

101

mean that Jacob had lost his faith in God. The earnest prayer recorded immediately afterwards indicates that this was not so (verses 9-12). He took what appeared to him to be the necessary precautions and then made his prayer to God. Surely this is how many of us would behave when faced by the uncertainties of the future. God, however, would put him to the proof and seek to draw out of him a deeper and more profound understanding of what trust in the Almighty involved. Having sent his wives and children and all his company over the brook Jabbok, the record tells us:

"Jacob was left alone; and there wrestled a man with him until the breaking of the day." (verse 24)

"He wept and made supplication ..."

He was alone with God, and the man who wrestled with him was none other than an angel of God. We usually think of wrestling as one man seeking to throw the other to the ground, but however the contest started it developed into a situation where Jacob, having clasped his hands about the angel, simply would not let him go. He came to an appreciation that in the fears and uncertainties that had overtaken him he was in fact wrestling with God, so he would not let Him go unless He blessed him (verse 26). The prophet Hosea throws further light on the incident, for he tells us:

"... he had power with God: yea, he had power over the angel, and prevailed: he wept, and made supplication unto him." (12:3,4)

The words of Hosea bring home to us the intensity of the situation in which Jacob found himself. It developed into a profound spiritual experience in which all the circumstances of his life at that time became, as it were, focussed in this one event. Jacob undoubtedly believed that the angel with whom he wrestled represented God, whose providential hand was working in his life for his good. So he would not let Him go; he clung to Him, weeping and praying for the promised blessing. The angel changed his name to Israel, a prince with God, and in the strength of that blessing he went forth into the dawn of a new day (Genesis 32:31).

Gethsemane

We cannot but think of the Lord Jesus in the Garden of Gethsemane who being in an agony prayed more earnestly (Luke 22:44). He too was alone with God for he was withdrawn "about a stone's cast" from the disciples (verse 41). The Lord Jesus was wrestling with the awful prospect of the cross and in the anguish of his soul he also was striving and agonising with God who strengthened him by an angelic messenger (verse 43):

"Who in the days of his flesh, when he had offered up prayers and supplications with strong crying and tears unto him that was able to save him out of death, and was heard in that he feared."

(Hebrews 5:7 with RV margin)

We know that the experience of the Lord Jesus in Gethsemane was not unique, for he "ofttimes resorted thither" (John18:2). Throughout his life he carried the dreadful burden of the cross and many must have been the occasions when with crying and tears he made supplication to his Father whom he knew was able to save him out of death.

As with Jacob and the Lord Jesus we too wrestle with God in all the circumstances of our lives. It is only when we are alone with Him that with strong crying and tears we can make our requests known unto Him; cling to Him, never let Him go until He blesses us and, by His grace, we emerge from the dark night of sin and sorrow and know the joy of that morning without clouds.

20

INTERPRETING BIBLE PROPHECY

IT is sometimes said of certain prophecies that they have secondary or double meanings. While we usually understand what is meant when such language is used, we believe that this is not the correct perspective. We suggest that a more accurate description of such prophecies would be to say that they have recurring fulfilments.

In a sense such prophecies are timeless: they are statements of God's intent. They tell us how He will react to certain situations whenever, and however many times, they might arise. Again, a prophecy might speak of an attitude adopted towards a certain people, that because it describes a perpetual expression of feeling, can have in the passage of time a repeated, not to say, a continuous fulfilment. The point we are making is best illustrated by looking at some examples from the Old Testament.

"A nation of fierce countenance"
Deuteronomy 28 is a classic example of this principle of interpretation of Bible prophecy. The chapter with its litany of curses that were to befall the people of Israel if they were unfaithful to their God, describes the various circumstances that would overtake them. These were not specific to one situation but were a warning to them of the way in which God would react to their wickedness if they departed from His ways (see verses 15-45).

There is, however, reference made to one judgement in particular that we can trace through the pages of scripture:

"The LORD shall bring a nation against thee from far, from the end of the earth, as swift as the eagle flieth; a nation whose tongue thou shalt not understand; a nation of fierce countenance, which shall not regard the person of the old, nor shew favour to the young." (verses 49,50)

They were to be invaded by a nation from afar, who like the eagle would swoop down upon them. They would not understand their language, and they would ruthlessly devastate their cities showing no pity either to young or old. The inability to understand their speech is something that brings home to us the terror which their cruelty and antagonism would have engendered, for there would be no means of communication and no comprehension of that which was overtaking them. The nation is described as being "of fierce countenance". Literally the word translated "fierce" means 'strong, hard or inflexible' (*Cambridge Bible*).

Successive aggressors

This prophecy of Deuteronomy 28 becomes the basis of the actions of successive aggressors whom God brought upon His people because of their disobedience. God's reaction to such a situation as that described in the prophecy was always the same. Thus it is recorded of Assyria:

"He shall come as an eagle against the house of the LORD." (Hosea 8:1)

"And he will lift up an ensign to the nations from far, and will hiss unto him from the end of the earth: and, behold, he shall come with speed swiftly." (Isaiah 5:27, with RV margin)

"Thou shalt not see a fierce people, a people of a deeper speech than thou canst perceive; of a stammering tongue that thou canst not understand." (Isaiah 33:19)

In similar fashion it is recorded of the Babylonians:

"Lo, I will bring a nation upon you from far, O house of Israel, saith the LORD: it is a mighty nation, it is an ancient nation, a nation whose language thou knowest not, neither understandest what they say."
(Jeremiah 5:15)

"Behold ye among the heathen, and regard, and wonder marvellously: for I will work a work in your days, which ye will not believe, though it be told you. For, lo, I raise up the Chaldeans, that bitter and hasty nation, which shall march through the breadth of the land, to possess the dwellingplaces that are not theirs. They are terrible and dreadful: their judgment and their dignity shall proceed of themselves. Their horses also are swifter than the leopards, and are more fierce than the evening wolves: and their horsemen shall spread themselves, and their horsemen shall come from far: they shall fly as the eagle that hasteth to eat." (Habakkuk 1:5-8)

This passage from Habakkuk is particularly interesting as the prophet is clearly referring to the Babylonians. Yet in the New Testament it is quoted by the Apostle Paul in his address to the Jews at Antioch in Pisidia, indicating that the prophecy was capable of yet another fulfilment:

"Beware therefore, lest that come upon you, which is spoken of in the prophets; Behold, ye despisers, and wonder, and perish: for I work a work in your days, a work which ye shall in no wise believe, though a man declare it unto you." (Acts 13:40,41)

In this instance it must surely be a warning of the danger in which the nation stood from the power of Rome, which was eventually the agent used by God to scatter His people throughout the earth. There remain, of course, the words of the prophet Daniel regarding the little horn of the goat, which lie beyond the scope of this study to consider.

A confederacy of nations

Psalm 83 speaks of a confederacy of nations, bound together in common cause, to destroy the nation of

Israel and to blot out their name from the earth (verses 4,5). Ten nations are mentioned and all of them, with one exception, are of Arab extraction, living in close proximity to the nation of Israel. They are all people who 'rubbed shoulders' with Israel throughout their history in the land. There is some difference of opinion as to when this psalm was written, but it would appear that the most likely possibility is that which relates it to the days of Jehoshaphat when a confederacy of Arab nations threatened Judah (2 Chronicles 20).

Moab and Ammon (i.e., the children of Lot) and "with them other beside" (2 Chronicles 20:1), together with the Edomites (verse 10), present a great multitude and strike fear into the heart of all Judah. Jehoshaphat and the people present themselves before the Lord and the words of the king's prayer strike a chord with the language of the psalm (2 Chronicles 20:5-12). Consider this host, says Jehoshaphat, for:

"Behold, I say, how they reward us, to come to cast us out of thy possession, which thou hast given us to inherit. O our God, wilt thou not judge them? for we have no might against this great company that cometh against us: neither know we what to do: but our eyes are upon thee."   (verses 11,12)

"A perpetual hatred"

Although the language of the psalm is different, the thoughts expressed are precisely the same. Now whether or not the suggested historical background is correct, the fact remains that the antagonism shown towards the people of Israel is, in the sense we have suggested, timeless, for it spans the history of these people to the present time. The ten nations enumerated are: the Ishmaelites, Moab, the Hagarenes, Gebal, Ammon, Amalek, Tyre, the Philistines, Edom and Assur.

It is an interesting reflection on the relationship between Israel and their Arab neighbours that, the days of Jehoshaphat aside, the surrounding nations are never the main aggressors; but rather like birds of prey, quick to offer assistance and feed on the carcass of

Israel as the power from the north accomplished that which they were unable to achieve in their own strength. Again, not all of the nations listed need to be involved at any one time, for what the psalm presents us with is the totality of their hatred and opposition towards their brother Israel.

Thus it was in the days of Nebuchadnezzar, for Edom in particular took advantage of Judah's distress. Ezekiel speaks of her "perpetual hatred" (35:5) and other prophets speak of her cruelty and swiftness to seek benefit from Israel's loss (see Obadiah verses 10,14; Psalm 137:7-9 etc.). Particularly interesting in this connection is the section of Ezekiel's prophecy that deals with God's judgements on the nations surrounding Israel. In chapter 25 we have reference to Ammon (verses 2-6), Moab (verses 8-12), Edom (verses 12-14) and the Philistines (verse 15). In chapters 26 to 28 we have a more detailed description of the judgement upon Tyre. This section opens with the words:

> "And it came to pass in the eleventh year, in the first day of the month, that the word of the LORD came unto me, saying, Son of man, because that Tyrus hath said against Jerusalem, Aha, she is broken that was the gates of the people: she is turned unto me: I shall be replenished, now she is laid waste."　　　　　　　　　　　　　　　　　(26:1,2)

The eleventh year was, of course, the last year of Zedekiah's reign. It was the year in which the two-year siege of the city by Nebuchadnezzar came to an end and the city was broken up, the temple destroyed and the people carried away captive (see 2 Kings 25).

All of these nations, Ammon, Moab, Edom, the Philistines and Tyre are among the nations listed in Psalm 83, and all of them rejoiced in the calamity that had overtaken Israel.

Perhaps the most remarkable fulfilment of the psalm has been in our own days with the establishment of the State of Israel. Most of the territory once occupied by these ancient nations is now held by Arab states, who are united together by one thing only – their hatred of Israel and their determination to cut them off from being a nation.

As we look with anticipation to the coming of the Lord Jesus we do well to remember that we have the authority of scripture to assure us that the 'peace process' is a sham: the "perpetual hatred" remains. The ultimate end these nations seek is unchanged and the psalm has a continuing fulfilment.

Psalm 2

The theme of the second psalm, spoken "by the mouth of thy servant David" (Acts 4:25), is drawn from the covenant that God made with David when He promised the everlasting stability of his throne and kingdom through one that He should raise up, to whom He would be a Father and who would be His Son (1 Chronicles 17:11,14).

The psalm clearly speaks of the future, but if it had an historical background then surely there is only one period in David's life to which it could refer. It is the period at the very end of his days when Solomon was anointed king. It was a time when various factions sought to take advantage of the situation to promote their own ambitions. David himself was left under no illusion as to the divine choice:

> "And of all my sons (for the LORD hath given me many sons), he hath chosen Solomon my son to sit upon the throne of the kingdom of the LORD over Israel. And he said unto me, Solomon thy son, he shall build my house and my courts: for I have chosen him to be my son, and I will be his father."
>
> (1 Chronicles 28:5,6)

"He that sitteth in the heavens shall laugh"

Of course, the grand theme of the psalm far transcends any incipient fulfilment that it might have had in the experiences of Solomon. It declares for all succeeding generations the immutability of God's purpose and the utter futility of all human endeavours to frustrate His pleasure. Here is the true significance of the psalm and it gives us yet another wonderful insight into the recurring nature of some Bible prophecies. Because God never changes, He always reacts to certain situations, which have a common factor, in the same way. Thus whenever the nations rage, and men are confederate together to rebel and to exalt themselves "against the LORD, and against his anointed", their efforts are doomed to failure, for "he that sitteth in the heavens shall laugh: the LORD shall have them in derision ... Yet have I set my king upon my holy hill of Zion" (Psalm 2:1-6).

Thus, the psalm could have an incipient fulfilment in the life of Solomon when God confounded all the evil counsels of his enemies. It seems also to be relevant to the times of Hezekiah when Jerusalem was besieged by the Assyrian host. The king appears to have possessed the spiritual appreciation to grasp the significance of the psalm. His prayer and God's response to it in Isaiah 37 contain some obvious references to the song:

"Thou art the God, even thou alone, of all the kingdoms of the earth: thou hast made heaven and earth." (verse 16)

"Hear all the words of Sennacherib, which he hath sent to reproach the living God." (verse 17)

"Now therefore, O LORD our God, save us from his hand, that all the kingdoms of the earth may know that thou art the LORD, even thou only." (verse 20)

"This is the word which the LORD hath spoken concerning him [Sennacherib]; The virgin, the daughter of Zion, hath despised thee, and laughed thee to scorn." (verse 22)

"I know ... thy rage against me. Because thy rage against me, and thy tumult, is come up into mine ears ..." (verses 28,29)

See also Psalm 46 which is commonly accepted as referring to the same event:

"The heathen raged, the kingdoms were moved: he uttered his voice, the earth melted." (verse 6)

Perhaps the most remarkable application of the psalm is that made by the apostles in the Acts of the Apostles (4:23-30). It is doubtful that we, without the guidance of the Spirit, would ever have applied it in this way. What is significant about the apostles' prayer is the way in which they not only quote Psalm 2, but also pick up the reference from Isaiah 37 reproduced above:

"Lord, thou art God, which hast made heaven and earth." (verse 24)

The apostles then proceed to apply the words of David to the manner in which, acting from their own particular point of view, men were confederate together to crucify the Lord Jesus. Herod, Pilate, the Gentiles and the people of Israel were joined together to perform, unwittingly, what God's hand and counsel had determined before to be done. When the Lord Jesus died, that, they thought, was the end of him. The embarrassment he caused them, the threat to their way of life, the challenge that he presented – all gone, disposed of, leaving them free to pursue their own ways. But He that sits in the heavens laughed. The Lord had them in derision, for on the third day He raised the Lord Jesus from the dead. Thereby He gave an assurance to all men that He has fixed a day in which He will judge the world by that man whom He has appointed. A day will come when, in the face of all men's efforts to frustrate His purpose, God will say, "Yet have I set my king upon my holy hill of Zion".

The future

Further fulfilments of the psalm remain: first, when the Lord Jesus Christ returns to the earth and sits on the throne of his glory. Then all nations will recognise his sovereignty. But first the nations will rage, they will take counsel together, against the Lord and His anointed. They will, however, be impotent before the might and the power of God – unable to do anything to frustrate the fulfilment of His purpose. Revelation 19 refers to this time (verses 11-21) and the words of the psalm are quoted directly:

"And out of his mouth goeth a sharp sword, that with it he should smite the nations: *and he shall rule them with a rod of iron*: and he treadeth the winepress of the fierceness and wrath of Almighty God." (verse 15)

Concerning this time the Lord Jesus has given us an assurance that we shall share his dominion, for his promise to the ecclesia at Thyatira was:

"And he that overcometh, and keepeth my works unto the end, to him will I give power over the nations: and he shall rule them with a rod of iron; as the vessels of a potter shall they be broken to shivers: even as I received of my Father." (2:26,27)

There remains, of course, the final confrontation between God and human arrogance and rebellion at the end of the Millennium (20:7-9). Psalm 2 is not quoted in connection with this final conflict, but nevertheless we can be sure that here we have the final fulfilment of the words of the song for, afterwards, "God (will) be all in all" (1 Corinthians 15:28).

21

"LET YOUR LIGHT SO SHINE"

THERE are essentially two adjectives that are translated 'good' from the Greek of the New Testament in our Authorised Version. They are *agathos* and *kalos*. They both carry the idea of that which is intrinsically good, and in this respect they could be regarded as synonyms. However the second of the words has an added emphasis, for it signifies also that which is seen to be good because it is fair or lovely. In short, that which is beautiful or attractive both in the eyes of God and men. It is this word which the Lord Jesus used when he counselled us:

"Let your light so shine before men, that they may see your *good* works, and glorify your Father which is in heaven." (Matthew 5:16)

In other words the lives that we live should not repel men but rather attract them. As far as possible we should seek to live a life that, in the sight of men is blameless, that does not leave us open to the criticism of our contemporaries. We have to remember that the Truth and those who embrace it are always under a spotlight. We are on trial by the world and while we must never compromise our standards we must seek to live in such a manner that our lives will be admired for their spiritual beauty.

The Acts of the Apostles
The book of Acts provides us with some stirring examples. The commission that the Lord Jesus gave to the first disciples was:

"Ye shall be witnesses unto me both in Jerusalem, and in all Judaea, and in Samaria, and unto the uttermost part of the earth." (Acts 1:8)

It was as if the Lord said to them, 'By the words that you speak and by the lives that you live, you will be witnesses unto me' – and so indeed they were.

The description of the ecclesia at Jerusalem recorded in Acts 2 gives us a wonderful insight into the harmony that existed amongst them and the bond of love that united them together:

> "They continued stedfastly in the apostles' doctrine and fellowship, and in breaking of bread and prayers." (2:42)

> "And all that believed were together, and had all things common; and sold their possessions and goods, and parted them to all men, as every man had need." (verses 44,45)

The result was that recognising the attraction of their communal living they had favour with all the people (verse 47), or as one writer colloquially translates it, "everybody liked them". In the words of the Lord Jesus:

> "By this shall all men know that ye are my disciples, if ye have love one to another." (John 13:35)

Before the Council

Again, when Peter and John appeared before the Jewish Council such was the manner in which they conducted themselves before them that they were compelled to recognise the power of their witness:

> "When they saw the boldness of Peter and John, and perceived that they were unlearned and ignorant men, they marvelled; and they took knowledge of them, that they had been with Jesus." (Acts 4:13)

Such was the authority with which they spoke that the Council acknowledged that they were changed men. The courage they displayed was so impressive that they recognised the Lord Jesus Christ in their demeanour and in the spirit they showed. They were letting their light shine before men.

When Paul and Silas came to Philippi their teaching brought them into conflict with the owners of the slave girl with a spirit of divination. They in their turn roused

114

the people, and Paul and Silas were dragged before the magistrates who, after beating them, commanded them to be thrust into the innermost prison where their feet were made fast in the stocks. There, with their aching limbs and lacerated backs, in what humanly speaking was a most unpleasant situation, they gave a most impressive demonstration of their faith:

> "And at midnight Paul and Silas prayed, and sang praises unto God: and the prisoners heard them."
>
> (Acts 16:25)

The RV says that the prisoners "were listening", and what a difference that makes. We may hear the sound of singing but not be listening to it. We only begin to listen when the singing attracts our attention and arouses our interest. So the prisoners listened, and no doubt marvelled at the spirit of these men who could rise above their suffering and show joy in the midst of their affliction because of the wonder of their relationship with the Lord Jesus Christ.

Perhaps we can apply some later words of the apostle to the situation in Philippi:

> "Let the word of Christ dwell in you richly in all wisdom; teaching and admonishing one another in psalms and hymns and spiritual songs, singing with grace in your hearts to the Lord."   (Colossians 3:16)

Shipwreck

Finally when Paul was in the ship tossed by the ferocity of the wind and sea, with the impending shipwreck imminent, perceiving the lack of leadership he took charge of the situation. Realising how desperate was their need for food he persuaded them to take some meat, assuring them also that not a hair should fall from the head of any of them (Acts 27:33,34).

> "And when he had thus spoken, he took bread, and gave thanks to God in presence of them all: and when he had broken it, he began to eat. Then were they all of good cheer, and they also took some meat."
>
> (verses 35,36)

When we consider the type of men who were on the ship we realise the power of Paul's example. They were soldiers, sailors, prisoners: hard men, coarse men, and no doubt the air was filled with their cursing and swearing. Yet Paul stood forth in the presence of them all and surely in an unpretentious manner gave thanks for the food. The result of Paul's calm and reassuring manner was that they were all encouraged, recognising his trust in God.

It surely makes us ashamed to think that sometimes in far less intimidating situations we murmur: "Give your own thanks".

Conclusion

There is much by way of exhortation in the examples we have considered. The primary characteristic of them all is that they were spontaneous demonstrations of the apostles' faith. They did not act in this way because they were anxious to make an impression, but because that was the kind of people they were.

The Apostle Peter has words of wise counsel for us:

"Having your conversation honest among the Gentiles: that, whereas they speak against you as evildoers, they may by your good works, which they shall behold, glorify God in the day of visitation."

(1 Peter 2:12)

The word "honest" has changed its meaning down through the centuries. It did not have the same emphasis on that which is true that it carries today. The *Oxford Dictionary* tells us that it is derived from the Latin *honestus* which meant 'lovely'. We must live our lives in a way that is lovely. We must live the message we preach. Significantly the Greek word translated "honest" is the word *kalos* – that which is seen to be good, that which attracts rather than repels. Therefore, "Let your light so shine before men, that they may see your good works, and glorify your Father which is in heaven".

22

"ENOCH WAS TRANSLATED"

THERE are two characters in the early chapters of Genesis who are named Enoch. One is the son of Cain and the other the father of Methuselah and the great-grandfather of Noah.

Of the name, *Strong's Concordance* tells us that it is derived from a Hebrew word meaning 'to discipline' and it carries the idea of education. Thus the word is used in the book of Proverbs:

"Train up a child in the way he should go: and when he is old, he will not depart from it."   (22:6)

Of Cain's son we are told that his father built (literally, 'began to build') a city and called it after the name of his son (Genesis 4:17). Thus did Cain seek to perpetuate his name in the earth.

"Their inward thought is, that their houses shall continue for ever, and their dwelling places to all generations; they call their lands after their own names."   (Psalm 49:11)

Here is the foundation of the kingdom of men. Cain had a vision of a world in which human endeavour would be glorified and men's achievements esteemed; a world in which men like Nebuchadnezzar could say:

"Is not this great Babylon, that I have built?"
(Daniel 4:30)

To this end Cain recognised the need of training and education, for only thus could his dream of 'a better world to sin in' become a reality. So, in recognition of this he named his son Enoch.

How different were the circumstances of that other Enoch who was born into the godly line of Seth. Here too there was a recognition of the need of training but,

117

in the spirit of Proverbs, this man was trained in the ways of the Lord and became one of the most remarkable characters in the Old Testament, for it is recorded of him that he "walked with God" (Genesis 5:22). The Genesis record is brief for it tells us only that "he was not; for God took him" (verse 24). Concerning the phrase, "he was not", we remember that this was the way Joseph's brethren described their family situation:

> "Thy servants are twelve brethren, the sons of one man in the land of Canaan; and, behold, the youngest is this day with our father, and one is not."   (42:13)

It would appear from this expression that they were describing their brother Joseph as missing. From their father's perspective they were saying that he was lost and they did not know what had happened to him. So also Enoch vanished because God took him, and his contemporaries had no idea what had happened to him or where he might be.

The witness of Hebrews

As so often happens, our understanding of Old Testament scripture is enlarged by further revelation in the New Testament:

> "By faith Enoch was translated that he should not see death; and was not found, because God had translated him: for before his translation he had this testimony, that he pleased God. But without faith it is impossible to please him: for he that cometh to God must believe that he is, and that he is a rewarder of them that diligently seek him."   (Hebrews 11:5,6)

First of all we note that the conclusion we arrived at in Genesis that Enoch disappeared and that men had no knowledge of what had happened to him is strengthened by the words of Hebrews: "he was not found". In other words, men were looking for him but failed to find him.

The word "translated" has no mystical significance for the lexicons tell us that it means simply to be moved from one place to another. Genesis says that "God took him", so we conclude that God removed Enoch from his usual environment to some other place beyond the reach of his fellow men. The purpose of this transfer from one place to another was "that he should not see death". It is difficult to accept, as some have suggested, that Enoch was spared the fate that eventually befalls all mortal men and that he has been preserved in heaven since his translation. In fact the Epistle to the Hebrews tells us:

"These all died in faith, not having received the promises." (11:13)

Presumably Enoch would have been included amongst these. What then is the alternative?

The seventh from Adam

Jude enlarges our knowledge of the life of Enoch when he tells us in his epistle:

"And Enoch also, the seventh from Adam, prophesied of these, saying, Behold, the Lord cometh with ten thousands of his saints, to execute judgment upon all, and to convince all that are ungodly among them of all their ungodly deeds which they have ungodly committed, and of all their hard speeches which ungodly sinners have spoken against him."

(Jude 14,15)

Enoch then was a prophet and the words of Jude are not intended to convey the idea that he prophesied specifically of those false teachers that the apostle was indicting. The RV renders the passage: "And to these also Enoch, the seventh from Adam, prophesied." The words of Enoch were therefore relevant to ungodly men of every age, and when they were originally spoken they were directed against the wicked of his own generation.

The depravity and decadence of the times is indicated by the emphasis upon the word "ungodly". Genesis itself gives us an insight into the prophetic office that Enoch fulfilled when it tells us that he called his son 'Methuselah', for that name means, 'He dies and it is

119

sent' (*Fausset's Bible Dictionary*). Methuselah died in the year of the flood, so almost a thousand years before it came, Enoch had spoken of that judgement that was to come, although perhaps not specifically about a flood.

We have a further clue in the words of Jude when he speaks of the "hard speeches" that were uttered by the ungodly. Just as Enoch was the seventh from Adam in the godly line of Seth, so we find that in the line of Cain, those motivated by the thinking of the serpent, the seventh was Lamech who was almost certainly a contemporary of Enoch. He is best known to us by what is commonly known as his sword song:

"Hear my voice; ye wives of Lamech, hearken unto my speech: for I have slain a man for wounding me, and a young man for bruising me: if Cain shall be avenged sevenfold, truly Lamech seventy and sevenfold."   (Genesis 4:23,24, RV)

The words translated "wounding" and "bruising" describe the kind of injury that might be inflicted by striking with the fist; it is possible that the second word could refer to a verbal insult rather than a physical assault. Lamech's words, however, indicate, 'to run through with a sharp implement', hence his sword song. It is the proud boast of an arrogant man who delighted in bloodshed and violence: a man who was determined to avenge himself for every supposed insult and indignity inflicted upon him.

Lamech was almost certainly one of the original giants who became men of renown (Genesis 6:4). The word 'giant' in this context does not necessarily mean men of great stature. It is derived from a root which means 'to fall upon': hence men of violence who because of their prowess with the sword became "men of renown", or more accurately "men of name or reputation" who were known and feared because of their violent reaction to those who offended them in any way. Such a man was Lamech; and it was to such men that Enoch prophesied because of their evil works.

Given the reaction of Lamech towards those whom he felt had insulted him and did not show deference to his authority, established by the power of the sword, it is not difficult to imagine his response to the prophecy of Enoch. He would have sought to take his life. But from the violent death that Lamech, or his like would have imposed upon Enoch, God delivered him. He translated him that he should not see death at Lamech's hands, and though they searched for him diligently they were unsuccessful in their quest, for God took him and he was not found.

He pleased God

We often quote the sixth verse of Hebrews 11 to demonstrate the importance of faith. What is not always appreciated is that the verse is a continuation of the record of the faith shown by Enoch. "Before his translation he had this testimony, that he *pleased* God". The RV demonstrates the force of the word when it translates it, both in verses 5 and 6, as "well-pleasing". The intimacy of his relationship is indicated in Genesis where it was recorded of him that "he walked with God". So without faith it is impossible to be well-pleasing unto Him. He who seeks God must believe that He is; there must be a conviction of the reality of God and a confidence in the faithfulness of His promise that He will reward those that diligently seek Him. Enoch was numbered amongst such, and so the question is suggested, Was his deliverance from those who sought his life also linked to a reward for his faithfulness? Where might God have taken him? We are in the area of conjecture here, but it is hard to imagine that Enoch lived the rest of his life in complete isolation.

We remember that Cain also, before he wilfully went out from the presence of the Lord, lived under His protection. Is it possible that Enoch was taken to the Garden of Eden, or at least to the vicinity of that paradise of God, where this man who had walked with God would have enjoyed the fellowship and ministration of angels as he lived out the remainder of his mortal life?

It appears to the writer that this is a far more satisfying conclusion than to imagine that Enoch was transported to heaven, thereby escaping death which is the inevitable end of Adam's entire sin-stricken race.

23

"JUDGE NOT"

THE theme of making judgements in relation to others is one that sometimes causes confusion. For instance, the words of the Lord Jesus quoted from Matthew 7:1 which form the title of our consideration, are occasionally employed in a blanket fashion that seems to rule out any exercise of discrimination concerning the deeds of others. As we read scripture we must be aware that this cannot be true, for the same Lord that uttered these words also said on another occasion, "Judge righteous judgment" (John 7:24). A few verses further in this very seventh chapter of Matthew, the Lord advises us to "give not that which is holy unto the dogs, neither cast ye your pearls before swine" (verse 6). However we interpret these words, clearly we have to reach a decision as to whom the Lord meant by the words, "dogs" and "swine". Similarly, a little later in the chapter the Lord warns us of the danger of false prophets. His guidance is, "Wherefore by their fruits ye shall know them" (verse 20). In other words, by the exercise of judgement we shall recognise and reject them.

The wickedness of today's society provides us with another illustration. We know that Lot was "vexed (literally, 'tortured') with the filthy conversation of the wicked". He was tormented daily by their unrighteous acts. We can no more condone the evil that fills the world in which we live, than Lot could ignore the foul way of life of the men of his generation. We have a responsibility to witness and in the very nature of things this involves making judgements concerning the deeds of men.

The corporate judgement of the ecclesia

Again there are occasions when as ecclesias we have to make judgements about the behaviour of individual members. The first Epistle to the Corinthians provides us with a number of examples of the Apostle Paul's advice on the responsibility of the ecclesia to exercise its corporate judgement.

There was the case of the incestuous brother who had formed a relationship with his father's wife (1 Corinthians 5:1-5) and the apostle is moved to indignation because the ecclesia had failed to exercise proper responsibility in this matter. He judged them because of their failure to censure the brother who had behaved in such an inappropriate way. Although absent, he had judged as though he were present and urged them to come together in the same spirit and to put away from among them the perpetrator of this evil deed.

Similarly the apostle was concerned that in their anxiety to claim what they perceived to be their rights, brother was going to law with brother before the unbeliever (6:1-8). Properly they should have suffered themselves to be defrauded (verse 7), but if through circumstances or hard-heartedness they were not prepared to do so, then the matter was to be resolved within the ecclesia and judgement was to be made in an appropriate manner (verses 2-5).

Ecclesial responsibilities have not changed and we still have a duty, when situations arise that require our collective judgement, to exercise discernment in reaching an appropriate decision.

The guidance of the word

Of course, it hardly needs to be said that, where the teaching of scripture is involved, then we must endorse the authority of the word of God. In this respect we have an infallible guide and strictly speaking it is not we, but the scripture that judges the actions of men.

124

However, it is a universal human weakness that while we are able to apply scripture to others in this way, we can blithely turn a blind eye to our own failings. Herein lies the danger and again the scripture provides us with examples of human fallibility in the exercise of discretion and judgement.

Human weakness

In Genesis 38 we have the record of Judah's dealings with his daughter-in-law, Tamar. Following the deaths of Er and Onan (verses 1-10) Judah requests Tamar, the wife of Er, to remain in his house until Shelah, his third son, has reached an age of maturity so that he can raise up seed to his brethren. In process of time, Judah appears to have neglected his obligation to Tamar and she takes matters into her own hands. She disguises herself as a harlot and meets Judah in the way (verses 14-21). As a result of their liaison Tamar becomes pregnant and upon discovering her condition, Judah, moved to anger, would have put her to death. It is only when she produces the tokens given to her by Judah that he recognises the perfidiousness of his actions and confesses, "She hath been more righteous than I" (verses 25,26). Judah's double standards were revealed. He judged Tamar by a different measure from the one he applied to himself. So often it is the case. Men treat their own secret sins as though they had never been committed, while condemning the same sins that have been openly revealed in others.

Perhaps an even more striking example is that of David when confronted by the prophet Nathan over his sin in the matter of Bathsheba and Uriah the Hittite. Nathan's parable of the rich man and the poor man's little ewe lamb (2 Samuel 12:1-4) caused David to burn with anger: "The man that hath done this thing shall surely die", cried David, only to be struck with remorse at Nathan's response: "Thou art the man" (verses 5-7). The fact that such a man as David, a man after God's own heart, could deceive himself in such a way, is a salutary warning. It is dangerous to operate double standards: harshly judging others when we are guilty of the same things.

Both Judah and David were guilty of that which they condemned in others and the Apostle Paul expresses the truth of the matter in his indictment of the Jews generally in their hypocritical attitude to the law:

"Therefore thou art inexcusable, O man, whosoever thou art that judgest: for wherein thou judgest another, thou condemnest thyself; for thou that judgest doest the same things … And thinkest thou this, O man, that judgest them which do such things, and doest the same, that thou shalt escape the judgment of God?"

(Romans 2:1-3; see also verses 17-23)

The mote and the beam

The Lord Jesus highlighted this human failure when, with more than a touch of humour, he said:

"And why beholdest thou the mote that is in thy brother's eye, but considerest not the beam that is in thine own eye? Or how wilt thou say to thy brother, Let me pull out the mote out of thine eye; and, behold, a beam is in thine own eye? Thou hypocrite, first cast the beam out of thine own eye; and then shalt thou see clearly to cast out the mote out of thy brother's eye."

(Matthew 7:3-5)

The picture, which must surely have caused some amusement, is of a man with a plank of wood in his eye desperately striving to remove a twig out of his brother's eye.

The lesson is, of course, deadly serious. The one was oblivious of his own failing. Such was his self-esteem that he was blinded to his desperate need, yet nonetheless still anxious to put right the much smaller fault that he detected in his brother.

Luke's record of the Lord's words, uttered surely on a different occasion, has an interesting variation (6:41,42). The man with the beam in his eye speaks to his fellow disciple: "Brother, let me pull out the mote

126

that is in thine eye". So much depends upon the emphasis, the inflection of the voice. One wonders whether the word "brother" has an air of insincerity, a pretence of goodwill, for so much can be conveyed by the manner in which a word is spoken.

To despise one's brother

We return to the Lord's words in Matthew 7. The Greek verb is imperative: literally, "Be not judging". It describes a critical censorious spirit that is always seeing the bad and never looking for the good. *Vine's Expository Dictionary* says of the word, that it signifies 'to assume the office of a judge'. It describes the attitude that does not simply judge, in the sense of showing a discriminating or judicious spirit, but it goes further in that it also condemns. Herein lies the danger, for whereas we have an infallible guide in the scriptures to determine whether actions are right or wrong, we have no such guide in determining an individual's guilt. We cannot judge motives or the pressure of circumstances. God alone knows the hearts of men. He only knows the truth of the situation and the measure of the guilt or otherwise of the individual.

The Apostle Paul in writing his Epistle to the Romans has some telling observations to make in the context of judging one's brother over the question of eating of meats and the observance of days:

> "But why dost thou judge thy brother? or why doest thou set at nought thy brother? for we shall all stand before the judgment seat of Christ." (14:10)

Of the word translated "set at nought", *Strong's Concordance* says, "to make utterly nothing of, i.e., despise". Elsewhere it is translated as "contemptible" and the attitude expressed is indicative of that censorious spirit that the Lord condemned. Because his brother does not conform to his assessment of what is right or wrong in a particular situation, he judges him as nothing in the sight of God and unworthy of the kingdom of God. However, the reality is that we shall all

127

stand before the Judgement Seat of Christ to give account of ourselves to God.

There are some words of the Lord Jesus that emphasise the danger of judgements to which Paul referred:

"Ye have heard that it was said by them of old time, Thou shalt not kill; and whosoever shall kill shall be in danger of the judgment: but I say unto you, That whosoever is angry with his brother without a cause shall be in danger of the judgment: and whosoever shall say to his brother, Raca, shall be in danger of the council: but whosoever shall say, Thou fool, shall be in danger of hell fire." (Matthew 5:21,22)

There is a gradation of the offence committed and the level of responsibility to judgement.

The man who is angry with his brother without a cause has in his heart the seed that could grow into murder. He is responsible to the local court (see Deuteronomy 16:18). The man who says to his brother "Raca" openly despises his fellow. The word as indicated in the AV margin means 'vain fellow'. It describes a man of no substance. To regard a brother in such a way can only be possible when anger has hardened into a scornful dismissal of his worth and to do so would make a man responsible to the Council or Sanhedrin.

There is still, however, a further stage in the development of judging one's brother. To say, "Thou fool", is clearly a term of extreme moral opprobrium. It was not intended to describe a man's intellectual ability. Rather it is the fool of Proverbs, or Psalm 14:1 who has "said in his heart, There is no God". It is to regard him as utterly godless – unfit for the kingdom of God. To so judge is to make oneself responsible to the judgement of Gehenna – the final, eternal judgement of God, from which there is no escape.

Conclusion

How needful it is then to heed the counsel of the Lord Jesus not to be of a censorious and judgemental spirit, remembering also the need for a balanced approach, for there will always be occasions when the guidance of the word of God will lead us to judge the actions of an individual, but never the motives or the deep things of the heart which God alone knows. As several writers have expressed it: "We must be judicious without ever becoming judicial". We condemn the act but not the individual, for that is God's prerogative alone.

24

"MOSES MY SERVANT"

THE life of Moses can conveniently be divided into three periods of forty years. The first was spent in Pharaoh's court, the second in the land of Midian and the third leading God's people out of the land of Egypt to the borders of the Promised Land.

The birth of Moses
God had told Abraham that his seed would dwell for four hundred years in a strange land (Genesis 15:13), and as the end of that period drew near one would have anticipated an air of expectancy amongst the people. It appears, however, that they had become absorbed in the ways of the Egyptians and had even adopted the worship of their gods (see Joshua 24:14). As always there remained a faithful remnant and amongst these were Amram and Jochebed of the tribe of Levi.

The record of Moses' birth is brief and the words that "he was a goodly child" (Exodus 2:2) are given a special emphasis. Stephen describes him as "exceeding fair" (Acts 7:20, AV margin: "fair to God"). The Epistle to the Hebrews (11:23) says that "he was a proper child" ("proper" being the same Greek word as "fair" in Acts 7:20).

It is worthy of note that when special emphasis is placed on the birth and growth of a child it is usually because it has been as a result of divine revelation (as in the case of Samuel, Samson, John the Baptist, and the Lord Jesus Christ). It seems evident that Moses' parents had a conviction that this child was to play an important role in the deliverance of Israel from Egypt. It is possible that this was because there had been some kind of revelation either to them personally or to the people of Israel generally. How else are we to understand the words of Hebrews that "by faith" he was "hid three months of his parents because they saw he was a proper child"?

In Pharaoh's court

Of the forty years that Moses spent in Pharaoh's court the scripture tells us little. It is summed up in the words of Stephen in Acts 7:

> "And when he was cast out, Pharaoh's daughter took him up, and nourished him for her own son. And Moses was learned in all the wisdom of the Egyptians, and was mighty in words and in deeds."
>
> (verses 21,22)

We know that in those early formative years of his life Moses was nurtured and instructed by his mother and it was during this time that he learned of Israel's God, of the promises He had made and Moses came to regard himself as a man of destiny through whom God would deliver His people. Egypt was a great centre of culture and learning in that ancient world. He could therefore be classed as an intellectual. He was an eloquent man and a great military commander. Scripture tells us nothing of his exploits but Jewish tradition speaks of great victories against the Ethiopians in particular. Moses was a prince of the royal house of Egypt and the world lay at his feet. Even the highest position of all, the throne, might have been his. There can be little doubt that through his training in the Egyptian court Moses became convinced that this life he was experiencing was fitting him for the task of delivering his people.

Amongst his people

So when he was forty years of age it came into his heart to visit his people (Acts 7:23). It is important to appreciate that this was no casual visit, but it was a deliberate choice made, not by an impetuous youth, but by a mature man who publicly expressed his intention to be associated with his oppressed and downtrodden people. In effect he went and lived amongst them:

"By faith Moses, when he was come to years, refused to be called the son of Pharaoh's daughter; choosing rather to suffer affliction with the people of God, than to enjoy the pleasures of sin for a season; esteeming the reproach of Christ greater riches than the treasures in Egypt: for he had respect unto the recompence of the reward. By faith he forsook Egypt, not fearing the wrath of the king; for he endured, as seeing him who is invisible." (Hebrews 11:24-27)

Note the words, "Choosing to suffer affliction", "the reproach of Christ", "not fearing the wrath of the king" and "he endured". Moses turned his back on all that Egypt had to offer. He refused to accept the royal patronage that would have secured for him all the riches and honour the world could give. Instead he chose to live amongst his people and share their affliction. We can appreciate how this behaviour would have mystified the Egyptians and then outraged them. They would regard him as having brought disgrace on the royal house and Pharaoh's anger must have burned hot against him. No doubt it was only his former eminence in the royal court that prevented them from taking more decisive action.

"He had respect unto the recompence of the reward", or as the Revised Standard Version renders it, "he looked to the reward". The Greek term conveys the idea "to look away, or to turn one's attention from everything that might distract and to fix the gaze on one thing alone" (Barclay, *New Testament Words*). Moses endured, seeing beyond the present material things of that world to the eternal things associated with God's kingdom, ever aware of the reality of the invisible God. All this he did with a conviction that by his hand God would deliver His people and that his training in the royal household had fitted him for this task.

Thus when Moses saw an Egyptian assaulting one of his brethren and slew him, he felt that his action would have acted as a rallying call to the men of Israel to accept him as leader and to rise up against their oppressors. His attempt to arbitrate between the two Israelites who fought with each other convinced him that this was not to be. "Who made thee a prince and a judge over us?" was the taunt that was flung at him and now Moses was forced to flee, for Pharaoh sought to kill him. A common citizen would surely have been summarily executed but Moses remained a prince of the royal house, and even at this juncture Pharaoh had to seek a suitable way to rid himself of this troublesome fellow. The lesson, however, is clear: this people would not be delivered by human might and ability. It would be in God's time and by God's hand. Israel was not ready to be delivered and Moses had not yet been fitted for the task. Many years were to pass before the divine training prepared him for the work and perhaps, puzzled and perplexed, he came into the land of Midian to await the call to rise up and return to Egypt.

In the land of Midian

For forty long years Moses remained in the land of Midian. His father-in-law Jethro may have been a direct descendant of Abraham through his wife Keturah and Midian their son (Genesis 25:1,2). It is possible therefore, that he was a worshipper of the one true God and consequently Moses would have had an affinity with him and with his family. Nevertheless, Moses must still have been waiting for the time when God would send him back to Egypt to deliver His people.

We know this because he never truly settled in this land and when his first son was born, in token of the fact, he called him Gershom (AV margin, "a stranger here"). It was during these years of waiting that God prepared him for that arduous task that lay before him. If nothing else, he must have learned the quality of patience and the importance of waiting on God for His guidance and instruction.

133

The burning bush

So it was that as he watched the flock of his father-in-law, he saw the bush that burned with fire and was not consumed (Exodus 3:1,2). The fire represented the presence of God and out of the bush He spoke to Moses. God said:

> "Come now therefore, and I will send thee unto Pharaoh, that thou mayest bring forth my people the children of Israel out of Egypt."   (verse 10)

The response of Moses to the divine call is in complete contrast to the bold assertive man of forty years before. "Who am I?" he asks, to be given this responsibility. He needs the assurance that God will be with him and five times in chapter 3 the words, "I have sent thee" are used, emphasising the truth that Moses came not in his own strength but as the representative of the God of Israel. In Exodus 4, perhaps remembering their previous attitude, Moses protests that his people will not believe him or listen to what he has to say and God graciously gives him three signs to reassure him. Most surprisingly of all, this man, once mighty in word and deed, once renowned for his eloquence, now claims, "O my Lord, I am not eloquent ... but I am slow of speech, and of a slow tongue" (Exodus 4:10). God appoints Aaron to speak on his behalf – clearly it was not Moses who would deliver this people, but the God of Israel.

Now we might infer from Moses' reluctance to undertake the work to which God had called him, that he was not really a strong character. That would be a great mistake. His appearances before Pharaoh and his leadership of the children of Israel reveal him to be, the Lord Jesus apart, one of the greatest men in the sight of God who has ever lived. When Aaron and Miriam spoke against him, he had this testimony:

> "My servant Moses ... is faithful in all mine house. With him will I speak mouth to mouth, even apparently, and not in dark speeches: and the

134

similitude of the LORD shall he behold."

(Numbers 12:7,8)

It is in this context of the rebellious spirit of Aaron and Miriam that Moses is described as "very meek, above all the men that were upon the face of the earth" (verse 3). His reaction to their jealousy reflects the true spirit of the man, for he prays to God to heal Miriam of her leprosy. He shows a concern for them both that characterised this period of his life. He bears no resentment, shows no bitterness but demonstrates a spirit of forgiveness that reveals him as a man who thought nothing of his own glory and importance. His primary concern was for the honour of the God he served and for the welfare of the people that had been entrusted to his care. Moses showed a spirit of patience, tenderness, longsuffering, perseverance and endurance that has surely never been surpassed in any except the Lord Jesus Christ.

We have a lovely insight into this spirit in Numbers chapter 11. Moses is told that Eldad and Medad prophesied in the camp and Joshua, jealous for the honour of his master, cries to him to rebuke them. With the gentlest of rebukes Moses responds:

"Enviest thou for my sake? would God that all the LORD's people were prophets, and that the LORD would put his spirit upon them!" (verse 29)

The golden calf

Moses' intercession on behalf of the people of Israel, and Aaron in particular, is breathtaking in its subjugation of self to the glory of God and the welfare of his brethren. Exodus 32 tells how because of the episode of the golden calf, God in his anger would have consumed this people and carried forward His purpose by making of Moses a great nation. Humanly speaking, who would have refused such an offer? After all, the people deserved such a punishment and what a tremendous privilege it would have been for Moses. By such means does God sometimes put His servants to the test, that those lovely qualities that lie undeveloped in them

135

might be revealed and matured. Moses' response is truly remarkable. His first thought is for the honour of God Himself. 'Do not give the Egyptians cause to reproach you', he pleads. 'Let them not say that you only brought them out to do them mischief, to consume them in the wilderness'. Secondly, he asks that God remember the covenant that He made with Abraham, Isaac and Jacob to multiply their seed and give to them the land that He had promised. "And the LORD repented of the evil that he thought to do unto his people" (see Exodus 32:9-14).

What is significant, however, is what the record in Exodus does not tell us. Moses comments on these events in the book of Deuteronomy (9:11-25) and reveals the very real nature of the crisis that occurred. It becomes evident that the anger of the Lord was first kindled against Israel while Moses was still in the mount. It is there that He declares His intention to destroy this people and make of Moses a great nation. At God's command Moses takes the two tables of stone and descends from the mount to the camp. Seeing the golden calf and casting the two tables of stone to the ground he breaks them in the sight of all the people. Moses is afraid because of the fierce anger of the Lord and in an endeavour to intercede on behalf of the people he prostrates himself on the ground for forty days and forty nights, neither eating bread nor drinking water. He tells us also that at that time the Lord was very angry with Aaron and would have destroyed him, but Moses pleaded on his behalf and God forgave his sin and the sin of the people. It is hard for us to grasp the burden of responsibility that Moses took upon himself in pleading in this way, but perhaps even Deuteronomy does not give us the full picture. In Psalm 106 we have a commentary on Israel's behaviour at the time of the exodus and referring to this incident the Psalmist says:

"Therefore he said that he would destroy them, had not Moses his chosen stood before him in the breach, to turn away his wrath, lest he should destroy them." (verse 23)

Moses stood in the breach

These words are truly staggering in their implication. In Exodus 19 God gave strict instructions about how the people and the priests were to conduct themselves, so that God did not break through and destroy them. Literally the idea is that God might make a breach in the protective wall that surrounded them and break through in anger and destroy them. This is what happened to Uzzah when he touched the ark. God made a breach upon him and in His anger broke forth upon him (2 Samuel 6:8). Such was the anger of God towards Israel's idolatry, so imminent were His judgements, that the breach had been made. He was about to break forth but Moses stood in the breach and turned away His anger. It is hard to find words to describe the boldness of this action or to appreciate the understanding of the character of God that enabled him to make such a seemingly impulsive and dangerous decision, for thus Moses interceded on behalf of Israel.

Just how remarkable a man Moses was, is seen in the final episode of his life when God told him:

> "Because ye believed me not to sanctify me in the eyes of the children of Israel, therefore ye shall not bring this congregation into the land which I have given them." (Numbers 20:12)

What disappointment Moses must have felt. Yet amazingly there was no bitterness or resentment in his heart. His only thought was for this people that he had led for forty years:

> "Let the LORD, the God of the spirits of all flesh, set a man over the congregation, which may go out before them, and which may go in before them, and which may lead them out, and which may bring them in; that the congregation of the LORD be not as sheep that have no shepherd." (27:16,17)

He was a true shepherd and his primary thought was for the flock. In response to his plea God set Joshua over the people and to him was given charge to bring Israel into the promised land.

His relationship with God

Apart from the Lord Jesus, there is no other man who had such a close and intimate relationship with God. With him God spoke face to face as a man speaks with his friend. His great longing was to know God:

> "Now therefore, I pray thee, if I have found grace in thy sight, shew me now thy way, that I may know thee, that I may find grace in thy sight."
>
> (Exodus 33:13)

His request to see God's glory was graciously granted, for said God, "there is a place by me", and there hidden in the cleft of the rock, the Lord made all his glory to pass by and declared His name. We may not have the same intimacy of relationship that Moses enjoyed, but in the Lord Jesus we too can approach His throne of grace with boldness (Hebrews 10:19). We can also have a place by Him, a fellowship, that through His word gives us an insight into the character of God, that we also might come to know Him and with Moses might treasure those eternal things that He has promised to those who love Him.

25

JAMES, THE LORD'S BROTHER

THE Apostle Paul tells us that when he found it necessary to go to Jerusalem to make the acquaintance of Peter, he stayed with him for fifteen days. On this occasion he saw none of the other apostles save James, the Lord's brother (Galatians 1:18,19). This is, perhaps, an indication of the important position that James held in the ecclesia at Jerusalem.

The manner in which his authority was accepted is illustrated by the way in which he, with Peter, took command of the situation at the Council of Jerusalem when Paul and Barnabas had explained the success of their preaching to the Gentiles, and sought some clarification of the position of these Gentile believers in regard to the Law of Moses (Acts 15:6-29). The only other reference to James in the Acts of the Apostles is in Chapter 21, when Paul, visiting Jerusalem once more, accepts the advice of James and the assembled elders as to how he should best conduct himself amongst the Jews who were zealous of the law (verses 17-25).

The testimony of Josephus

Although we know nothing else regarding James from the Book of Acts, the Jewish historian Josephus knew of him and tells how he was held in such high regard among the Jews because of the manner of his living that he was known as "James the Just". He also writes of his death at the instigation of the Sadducees who, taking advantage of the absence of a Roman Governor, brought him before the Sanhedrin who sentenced him to be stoned. It is of interest to note that Josephus refers to him as "the brother of Jesus, who was called

Christ, whose name was James", thus confirming Paul's description of him in the Epistle to the Galatians.

The Gospel records

Now we know from our reading of the Gospel records that during his ministry the Lord's brethren did not believe on him. Indeed, on at least one occasion they were positively antagonistic towards him and would have taken him away by force, believing him to be mad (Mark 3:21, AV margin, "kinsmen"). The names of the family of Joseph and Mary are given by both Matthew and Mark:

> "And when he was come into his own country, he taught them in their synagogue, insomuch that they were astonished, and said, Whence hath this man this wisdom, and these mighty works? Is not this the carpenter's son? Is not his mother called Mary? And his brethren, James, and Joses, and Simon, and Judas? And his sisters, are they not all with us? Whence then hath this man all these things?"
>
> (Matthew 13:54-56; see also Mark 6:3)

These passages, of course, have been the subject of much controversy. The Roman Catholic Church, for instance, insists that the word "brethren" means no more than close relatives, in this case cousins. They adopt this point of view because of their desire to propagate the doctrine of the perpetual virginity of his mother, Mary.

Similarly, the highly regarded commentator, Lightfoot, developed the theory that the brothers and sisters were the children of Joseph from a previous marriage, Joseph assumedly being much older than Mary. This view has proved to be influential among commentators, many of whom follow Lightfoot's suggestion. This of course would have made James the stepbrother and not the half-brother of the Lord Jesus.

The cleansing of the temple

It will be recalled that when the Lord Jesus cleansed the temple at the beginning of his ministry, "his disciples remembered that it was written, The zeal of thine house hath eaten me up" (John 2:17). This is a quotation from Psalm 69 (verse 9), which is preceded by the declaration: "I am become a stranger unto my brethren, and an alien unto my mother's children."

Is it not reasonable to suppose, as Mark 3 records, that his kinsfolk thought him to be "beside himself" because they could not comprehend why he should have committed, what, to them, was a bewildering and shameful deed which they thought brought dishonour, not only upon him, but also on his family in the eyes of the rulers of the Jews? What is particularly significant, however, is that those with whom he was alienated by this act are described as his "*mother's* children", thus proving conclusively that they were, James included, the half-brothers and half-sisters of the Lord Jesus.

The Epistle of James

If, as we believe, the epistle that bears James' name was written by the Lord's brother, what an insight it gives us into the character of this man who might have been filled with a sense of his own importance given his close relationship after the flesh with the only begotten Son of God? However, he introduces himself to his readers as "James the servant (RV margin, "bondservant") of the Lord Jesus Christ" (1:1). He was to be thought of as the Master's slave and, significantly, after this introduction only on one other occasion does he refer to him by either name or title. In this passage he speaks of him as "our Lord Jesus Christ, the Lord of glory" (2:1), thus making himself one with his readers and having no pretensions to privilege. There was no attempt to take advantage of his relationship; he shows no expectation to be treated with respect and deference. To James who, during his ministry, had not found it in his heart to believe on him, he had now become "the glory", the word "Lord" not being in the original Greek.

Undoubtedly, the Lord's post-resurrectional appearance to James (1 Corinthians 15:7) must have had a profound effect upon him. The fact that he was

141

singled out in this way, however, was not just because he was the Lord's half-brother. He must surely have already begun to revise his thinking concerning the Lord Jesus, and the Lord who had lived with him in Nazareth must have been aware of the sterling qualities he possessed that were to make him such a powerful influence in the ecclesia at Jerusalem.

The witness of James

The question might be asked, 'Other than as a matter of interest, what benefit is all this information about James to us?' Well, if we reflect upon the fact that this man must have lived with the Lord Jesus for well over twenty years, what a testimony his belief is to everything that the Lord claimed to be. It is, we suggest, one of the great proofs of the Lord's real identity.

It is fascinating to think of the manner in which this man must have shared his life with the Lord Jesus. They ate their meals together; they worked together; they participated in all those activities that fall to brothers growing up together in a family relationship. How much could he have told of the Lord's early years? He knew all the intimate details. If there had been mischief leading to the sins of youth he would have known.

Against this background, his ultimate acceptance of the Lord Jesus as the only begotten Son of God, his recognition of him as his Lord and Saviour, is a most remarkable and powerful testimony to the veracity of the scriptural record. Having lived in such close proximity to his half-brother for so long it is astonishing to read his words, albeit under the power of inspiration, that he is "our Lord Jesus Christ, the Glory" – for he beheld his glory, the glory of the only begotten of the Father, full of grace and truth (see John 1:14).

26

DARE TO BE A DANIEL

THE great theme of the prophecy of Daniel is the conflict between the kingdom of men and the kingdom of God. The assurance the book gives us is that God rules in the kingdom of men, that ultimately He will prevail over the pride and arrogance of men and establish His sovereignty over all the earth:

"And in the days of these kings shall the God of heaven set up a kingdom, which shall never be destroyed." (Daniel 2:44)

"And there was given him dominion, and glory, and a kingdom, that all people, nations, and languages, should serve him: his dominion is an everlasting dominion, which shall not pass away, and his kingdom that which shall not be destroyed." (7:14)

The two passages quoted above emphasise God's ultimate victory over all the pretensions of men to maintain their dominion over the earth. The first is against the background of Nebuchadnezzar's dream of a great image in human form that represented the kingdom of men in its constituent parts, describing the various historical stages through which it would pass before the establishment of God's kingdom. The second passage describes the same sequence of events, but now seen in vision by God's servant Daniel. The nature of the revelation is, however, quite different for now the nations are represented by four great beasts that arise out of the sea.

There is, of course, something very appropriate about the different perspectives. Nebuchadnezzar, a man filled with an inflated sense of his own importance, who gloried in human achievement (Daniel 4:30), saw the nations in human form:

"This great image, whose brightness was excellent, stood before thee; and the form thereof was terrible."

(2:31)

It was something to be admired and worshipped for it spoke to him of human power and dominion. However, Daniel in his vision saw the nations from the divine perspective – as the wild beasts of the earth who rend one another in their desire to achieve supremacy. In view of their experiences it must have been from this standpoint that Daniel and his three friends thought of the nation of their captivity.

Josiah's spiritual children

It is written of Josiah:

"And he did that which was right in the sight of the LORD, and walked in all the way of David his father, and turned not aside to the right hand or to the left."

(2 Kings 22:2)

It is surprising therefore to discover that all of his sons, and his grandson, who sat on the throne of Judah are described as wicked men (Jehoahaz, Jehoiakim, Jehoiachin, and Zedekiah). It is evident from the rapid decline in the faithfulness of the people that it was only the force of Josiah's personality and the power of his example that maintained what must have been, generally speaking, a superficial and outward form of righteousness. Evidently his children shared the people's lack of enthusiasm for the things of God and Josiah's death gave them the opportunity to indulge themselves in their own ways.

It was in the third year of the reign of Jehoiakim that Nebuchadnezzar besieged Jerusalem and gave commandment that certain of the children of Israel, of the king's seed and of the princes, were to be brought to Babylon, presumably to serve in the diplomatic service of the king. This was only three years after the death of Josiah and among them were Daniel, Hananiah, Mishael and Azariah who evidently had been brought up in the royal court of Judah. They had been influenced by Josiah and whereas his natural children had not followed his example, these four men were his spiritual children, who through the ages have provided a pattern of behaviour for godly men and women in the face of all the pressures the world brings to bear on them.

Surely there is a word of comfort here for those brethren and sisters who have struggled to bring up their children in the fear of the Lord, only to see them turn away from the Truth as they come to an age of maturity. Perhaps they can take comfort also in their spiritual children, those in the ecclesia that they have influenced by their example and dedication to the Lord Jesus.

Shinar and the Chaldeans

When Jehoiakim was given into the hand of Nebuchadnezzar, the Babylonian king not only took choice young men to serve him but also, as part of the spoil, he took of the vessels of the house of God which he brought into the land of Shinar to the house of his god (Daniel 1:2). Shinar was where Nimrod established the kingdom of Babel (Genesis 10:10); it was where men would have built a tower, that their name might be remembered in the earth (11:2). This place was synonymous with antagonism towards God. Here wickedness flourished and righteousness was despised. As with the beast-like character of the kingdom, it posed a dreadful threat to any of God's children compelled to live in such an environment.

The danger was seen in the purpose of their training for the king's service. They were such as had ability in them to stand before the king, "and whom they might teach the learning and the tongue of the Chaldeans" (Daniel 1:4). In other words, they wanted to turn them into Chaldeans – men who spoke their language, adopted their culture, lived their way of life and merged into their society to such an extent that they could not be told apart from them. To this end, the names of Daniel and his companions were changed to Belteshazzar, Shadrach, Meshach and Abednego, all of

145

which incorporated the names of Babylonian gods. This, of course, is the pressure that the world brings to bear on us. In far less trying and distressing circumstances than those experienced by Daniel and his three friends, the world would have us adopt its way of speaking, embrace its aims and ambitions, and espouse its culture and traditions, so that we too are not only in the world but of it.

Daniel purposed in his heart not to defile himself with the king's meat. He was determined to preserve his integrity and identity as a member of the covenant people of God. By eastern standards to partake of the king's meat would have been to commit oneself to the gods to whom, almost certainly, it had been offered. It would have been interpreted as an act of friendship and association with all that Babylon stood for (in this connection see, for instance, Genesis 31:54 and Nehemiah 8:9-12). The reluctance of the prince of the eunuchs to allow Daniel to prepare and eat his own food is understandable. However, God was at work for although we are not told precisely how it was accomplished, He had brought Daniel into "favour and tender love" with this man (Daniel 1:9).

We too can be assured that whenever we determine in our hearts to make a stand for that which is right, to maintain our identity, God will be at work to enable us to retain our integrity before Him.

The golden image

Daniel chapter 3 describes the trial of Shadrach, Meshach and Abednego in particular. Having erected an image of gold, Nebuchadnezzar calls all the various officials from the differing provinces of his empire to celebrate the dedication of the image (verses 2,3). The command of the king was that all people, nations and languages should bow down and worship the image at the appointed time, indicated by the playing of the assembled musicians (verses 4,5). Failure to do so would result in being "cast into the midst of a burning fiery furnace". It is important to appreciate the purpose

146

of the golden image. The command to worship it encompassed every part of Nebuchadnezzar's empire. It was an attempt to establish a universal religion that would bind together in common cause the divergent parts of his dominion. Its aim was not only religious but it had also a political dimension, and despots have always recognised the danger of allowing men freedom of thought. The classic example is the beast of the earth in Revelation 13 whose purpose was that any who would not worship the image of the beast should be killed (verses 12-17). This, of course, found expression historically in the Holy Roman Empire and the tyranny of the Papacy.

Faced with the commandment of the king, Daniel's three friends had no option but to refuse to obey. The result was that the king in his rage had them brought before him to give an account of themselves. Their response is an example of a truly remarkable faith:

"If it be so, our God whom we serve is able to deliver us from the burning fiery furnace, and he will deliver us out of thine hand, O king. But if not, be it known unto thee, O king, that we will not serve thy gods, nor worship the golden image which thou hast set up."   (Daniel 3:17,18)

Here was wonderful trust to believe that their God was able to deliver them out of the hand of this despotic man. But even more amazing – revealing an astounding faith in the authority and sovereignty of their God – is their acknowledgment that it might not be God's will to deliver them. If that should be the case, they were determined that the king should know that they still would not bow down and worship his golden image.

Here we see true confidence in God: an acknowledgment of His sovereign care, appreciating that although God is able to deliver in the most desperate of situations, sometimes, in His wisdom, He does not do so – not simply to put our faith to the test, but for our eternal well-being. The trust of Daniel's three friends stands as an example to us of the need to

147

be able to say in all the circumstances of life, "Not my will, but thine, be done".

The lions' den

Daniel chapter 6 provides us with our final example. Daniel, now an old man (certainly over eighty years old), distinguished himself above all the presidents and princes to such an extent that Darius thought to set him over the whole realm (verse 3). The consequence was that they were eaten up with jealousy and sought an opportunity to discredit him in the eyes of the king. However, such was his faithfulness that they could find no fault in him (verse 4).

Nevertheless, they knew their man. They had come to appreciate that Daniel's commitment to his God was such that he would allow nothing to detract from his service to Him or to interfere with his worship. So they conspired together to persuade Darius to issue a decree that if one were to ask a petition of any, other than the king, for the space of thirty days, then he should be cast into a den of lions. They knew that Daniel could not comply with such a command. We read:

> "When Daniel knew that the writing was signed, he went into his house; and his windows being open in his chamber towards Jerusalem, he kneeled upon his knees three times a day, and prayed, and gave thanks before his God, as he did aforetime."
>
> (verse 10)

Daniel was not prepared to compromise. He could have argued that he did not have to stop praying – only ensure that he was not seen to pray. In any case, it was only for thirty days and then he could resume his normal devotions without incurring the anger of the king. Faithful Daniel could see no grounds for deferring to a human monarch at the expense of his God. Again, he stands as a wonderful example to us as we feel the pressures that the world exerts, of single-minded devotion and commitment to our God.

Conclusion

Daniel and his three friends, in far more dangerous and difficult circumstances than we can ever imagine finding ourselves, provide us with the most stirring examples of how we should seek to withstand the influences of the world in which we live. "Dare to be a Daniel" – that is the challenge which faces us, for by faith, these men:

"… stopped the mouths of lions, quenched the violence of fire, escaped the edge of the sword, out of weakness were made strong." (Hebrews 11:33,34)

27

"BE YE DOERS OF THE WORD"

IN 1870, following a visit to Mumbles, then a village about five miles from Swansea (South Wales, UK), Brother Robert Roberts wrote in *The Christadelphian* that because of the nature of their employment (they were oyster fishers) the brethren and sisters there were able to enjoy the blessing of a meeting together, not only on a Sunday but also on one evening during the week. Strangely, for reasons that he did not elaborate on in detail, he regarded this as a mixed blessing. He pointed out that because of the pressures of employment and business, few, if any, other ecclesias were able to meet in this way.

Opportunities to meet together

In short, most ecclesias met only on a Sunday and did not have the opportunity that we take so easily for granted of enjoying a mid-week Bible Class. It is a searching thought and worthy of serious reflection that some, in neglecting these meetings, are failing to appreciate the privilege we have been afforded by God in having these opportunities, denied to previous generations.

However, for many larger ecclesias it is not just the Bible Class but also the Mutual Improvement Class, the Youth Circle, the Sisters' Class and perhaps other meetings as well – some held on a more informal basis. This means that some brethren and sisters can be out almost every evening of the week attending some form of Bible-related activity.

But even this is not the end of the story, for on Saturdays and weekends in most parts of the UK, there are Fraternal Gatherings, Study Days, Family Days,

Youth Gatherings etc., not to forget the week-long Bible Schools. We have developed a culture, based upon the study of the word of God, that many brethren and sisters have espoused with great zeal. We can only imagine that Brother Roberts, given his remarks referred to above, would be dumbfounded at the change in our ecclesial life. Indeed, the change from only fifty years ago is still quite staggering.

These activities have only been made possible by the tremendous changes in social conditions enjoyed in the Western world, and it would be wrong to criticise the way in which brethren and sisters have taken advantage of these changes to use their free time in the study of the word of God. Yet surely a warning note is appropriate.

"Not hearers only"

We must never forget that the primary purpose of Bible study is not just to provide mental excitement – a kind of intellectual stimulation that is an end in itself. Our reading of God's word and the time we spend meditating upon it, must produce a love of God's law. That word must become active, a living power in our lives that is manifested by the manner in which we become not just *hearers* but *doers* of the word.

While not underestimating the benefit we receive from our communal meetings around the word of God, surely the most productive study is that which we do on a personal basis. Given the number of meetings that we can attend, the question we need to ask is, 'Have we become a community of *hearers* ("forgetful hearers", James 1:25), perhaps neglecting the *doing* that is the primary purpose of our reading and meditation?'

This is not to discredit the meetings that are available to many of us. Indeed we need to encourage one another to attend, but how often we hear it said, "What a wonderful meeting it was", "How stimulating the addresses", "What good students of the word the speakers were". Again, no criticism of the speakers is intended. The warning is to the *hearers*, and it can be

151

summed up more adequately than any words of ours by the testimony of God to the prophet Ezekiel:

"Also, thou son of man, the children of thy people still are talking against thee by the walls and in the doors of the houses, and speak one to another, every one to his brother, saying, Come, I pray you, and hear what is the word that cometh forth from the LORD. And they come unto thee as the people cometh, and they sit before thee as my people, and *they hear thy words, but they will not do them*: for with their mouth they shew much love, but their heart goeth after their covetousness. And lo, thou art unto them as a very lovely song of one that hath a pleasant voice, and can play well on an instrument: *for they hear thy words, but they do them not.*"   (Ezekiel 33:30-32)

28

GOD'S GOOD GIFTS

IT sometimes appears when reading the Epistle of James that there is a lack of continuity in the way the various strands of thought are presented. This, however, is a false impression and careful consideration of the text will show that there is always a reason for the apparent changes of direction.

I wish you joy

The point is well illustrated by the first two verses of the Epistle:

> "James, a servant of God and of the Lord Jesus Christ, to the twelve tribes which are scattered abroad, greeting. My brethren, count it all joy when ye fall into divers temptations." (James 1:1,2)

The word "greeting" literally means, 'I wish you joy'. However, James was only too well aware that there were many of those to whom he was writing that were experiencing persecution. They were in situations of adversity because of the oppression of the rich and powerful. So in anticipation of the possible reaction of some of those who were afflicted in this way, James exhorts them to "count it all joy" (literally, 'every kind of joy') when they "fall into divers temptations". It should be noted that the same Greek word is translated both 'trials' and 'temptations'. Context must be our guide and, in this instance, 'trials' would appear to be the more appropriate word. As there were different kinds of trial, so also there were various kinds of joy to be found in them. Again, the word "fall" carries the significance of an unlooked for event – not something they had brought upon themselves by their own foolishness, but a happening that could truly be looked upon as the providential hand of God.

Of course there is no joy to be found in suffering for its own sake, so James would have them know the blessing of God's chastening hand:

> "Knowing this, that the trying of your faith worketh patience. But let patience have her perfect work, that ye might be perfect and entire wanting nothing." (verses 3,4)

The joy is to be found not in the suffering but in the knowledge of what God can accomplish through it. A faith that is never tried, that is never put to the test, is no faith at all. But, by putting us to the proof, God desires to produce in us that patience (i.e., endurance, perseverance) that, if it is allowed to reach its intended end will find us "perfect and entire wanting nothing". The sense of "perfect and entire" is illustrated by the use of the same Greek term to describe the lame man healed by Peter at the Beautiful Gate of the temple. By faith in the name of the Lord Jesus he stood before them in "perfect soundness" (Acts 3:16).

If any man lack wisdom

It might appear that here again we have an interruption in the train of thought, but actually there is a very close connection with what has gone before. The Revised Version makes this clear:

> "… that ye might be perfect and entire, lacking in nothing. But if any of you lack wisdom, let him ask of God, who giveth to all liberally and upbraideth not; and it shall be given him. But let him ask in faith, nothing doubting: for he that doubteth is like the surge of the sea driven by the wind and tossed." (James 1:4-6)

In the Greek text the same word, translated 'lacking' and 'lack', is used in verses 4 and 5. This is clear in the RV which makes the connection even clearer by the insertion of the conjunction, "but". Wisdom is the application of knowledge. So, says James, if any of you lack the ability to apply your knowledge in this way, if you find this concept of joy in suffering difficult – easy to accept intellectually but hard to make real in your experience – then you must ask God to help. Make it a matter of prayer and, if you ask in faith, God will respond.

It is important to emphasise the need for faith. We must believe that He is able to do it and, above all, we must want Him to do it. It is a matter of co-operation; the power of God's word and the interplay with the circumstances of life, controlled providentially, will produce the desired result, often in ways utterly beyond our comprehension.

When God gives, He does so freely and simply. Of the word translated "liberally", Strong says, "without self-seeking", and the emphasis is upon the unconditional nature of God's gifts if only we truly desire them and ask aright. What is true of wisdom is true also of all those other qualities of the life in Christ. If we are lacking in any respect and truly desire to live that life to which we have been called, then we can be confident that God will respond to our prayers. He "upbraideth not", that is, He does not give reproachfully or unwillingly, but from the overflowing fullness of His grace.

Again James emphasises the importance of believing that God is both willing and able to answer our prayers. There is no room for doubt (AV, "wavering"). It is said of the Greek verb that it is in the middle voice, inferring inner debate – that condition that sways first one way and then another without ever coming to a firm conviction. We have a powerful illustration of what James meant in the example of Abraham when the same word is used, but translated, "staggered not", in the context of faith in God's promise (Romans 4:20,21).

The witness of the Lord Jesus

We are reminded that during his ministry the Lord Jesus gave similar counsel to his disciples:

155

"Verily I say unto you, If ye have faith, and doubt not, ye shall not only do this which is done to the fig tree, but also if ye shall say unto this mountain, Be thou removed, and be thou cast into the sea; it shall be done. And all things, whatsoever ye shall ask in prayer, believing, ye shall receive."

(Matthew 21:21,22)

There are some things for which we can pray with absolute confidence, knowing that they are part of the revealed purpose of God. To do so is an expression of our longing for that purpose to be fulfilled. Thus, for example, we can pray for God's kingdom to come. The words of the Lord, however, seem to go further than that. The disciples had a problem in appreciating the meaning of the miracle of the barren fig tree. It had become in their minds a veritable mountain of doubt and uncertainty. By using the figure of the mountain the Lord Jesus was not speaking literally but using the figure of speech known as hyperbole – that is to exaggerate for the sake of effect or to make the point more powerfully. So the Lord Jesus is assuring us that our mountains can be removed; that is, our spiritual difficulties and problems can be overcome if only we ask in faith, for it is our Heavenly Father's desire that we should be transformed into the very image of His Son.

To be filled with doubt, however, is to be like the waves of the sea when they are thrown into turmoil by the blowing of the wind. God offers us a peace and tranquillity of spirit that grows out of the trust we have in Him to do all that is necessary for our salvation to be effected. To lack this kind of faith is to live in a continuous state of uncertainty; to be like the troubled sea when it cannot rest. Of such James says:

"For let not that man think that he shall receive any thing of the Lord. A double minded man is unstable in all his ways."   (1:7,8)

The *Cambridge Bible for Schools and Colleges* says of the Greek rendered "double minded" that before its use by James it was virtually unknown in other writings. It is as though he had coined the word himself. If so, it is almost certain that he had the Old Testament scriptures in his mind.

Speaking of those who put their trust in themselves, the Psalmist writes:

> "They speak vanity every one with his neighbour: with flattering lips and with a double heart do they speak." (Psalm 12:2)

The AV margin tells us that the Hebrew is "an heart and an heart" which admirably sums up the man who fails to cultivate that single-minded devotion in which God delights.

That God's gifts are freely available to us if we truly desire them and earnestly seek them is reinforced again by the words of the Lord Jesus:

> "Ask, and it shall be given you; seek, and ye shall find; knock, and it shall be opened unto you ... If ye then, being evil, know how to give good gifts unto your children, how much more shall your Father which is in heaven give good things to them that ask him?" (Matthew 7:7-11)

29

PAUL AND THE ECCLESIA AT EPHESUS

WHAT a challenge Paul faced at Ephesus – a pagan city dedicated to the worship of the goddess Diana. Paul spent three whole years there and such was the effectiveness of his preaching that all that dwelt in Asia, both Jews and Gentiles, heard the word concerning the Lord Jesus Christ (Acts 19:10). What a testimony to the power of the Gospel, for even an unbeliever, an opponent of everything that Paul stood for, was compelled to acknowledge the effect that his preaching had on all the province of Asia:

"For a certain man named Demetrius, a silversmith, which made silver shrines for Diana, brought no small gain unto the craftsmen; whom he called together with the workmen of like occupation, and said, Sirs, ye know that by this craft we have our wealth. Moreover ye see and hear, that not alone at Ephesus, but almost throughout all Asia, this Paul hath persuaded and turned away much people, saying that they be no gods, which are made with hands: so that not only this our craft is in danger to be set at nought; but also that the temple of the great goddess Diana should be despised, and her magnificence should be destroyed, whom all Asia and the world worshippeth." (verses 24-27)

Just how deep-rooted the worship of Diana was in this particular locality is difficult for us to appreciate. But we get an insight into the fervour of their worship when Demetrius provoked a riot and for the space of two hours they cried out, "Great is Diana of the Ephesians" (verse 34). We might say that the Lord Jesus Christ and Diana met in direct confrontation. Of course, Diana existed only in the minds of those who worshipped her. But the preaching of the Gospel is always directed towards winning the minds and the hearts of those who hear it and Diana had infiltrated into every aspect of the social and cultural life of the city. One of the facets of her influence was the sale of what were known as 'Ephesian letters'. These were charms that supposedly protected people from the evils of life. In this respect, Paul, in the name of the Lord Jesus, met them on their own ground, for:

> "God wrought special miracles by the hands of Paul: so that from his body were brought unto the sick handkerchiefs or aprons, and the diseases departed from them, and the evil spirits went out of them." (verses 11,12)

Their charms were totally ineffectual. They had no power to heal and before the evidence of the mighty power of God, men were won for the Lord Jesus.

The riches of His grace

The chief concern of Demetrius was that by the trade generated by the worship of Diana both he and his fellow craftsmen became very wealthy. Paul's preaching was hitting them where it hurt most – in their pockets. But it was not just the worshippers of Diana that were suffering loss. Those who embraced the hope of the Gospel recognised that it was necessary for them to sever all their previous association with the goddess and, where appropriate, to abandon the means by which they had formerly made their living – and a very lucrative source of income it must have been:

> "And many that believed came, and confessed, and shewed their deeds. Many of them also which used curious arts brought their books together, and burned them before all men: and they counted the price of them, and found it fifty thousand pieces of silver." (verses 18,19)

These were the tools of their trade; through their use they became rich. But the books themselves were extremely valuable and that the name of the Lord Jesus Christ might be magnified in the eyes of the people they

159

publicly demonstrated their faith and for his sake became poor.

Yet spiritually they were rich and the Apostle Paul emphasises this truth as he develops the theme of his epistle. They had "redemption through his blood, the forgiveness of sins, according to the riches of his grace" (Ephesians 1:7). For –

> "God who is rich in mercy ... hath quickened us together with Christ ... that in the ages to come he might shew the exceeding riches of his grace in his kindness toward us through Christ Jesus."
>
> (2:4-7; see also 1:18; 3:8,16)

God had compensated them for that which they had willingly sacrificed by pouring upon them the riches of His grace. Spiritual blessings had overflowed into their lives from the abundance of God's goodness.

There was, however, another factor which led Paul to emphasise the divine riches available to those who committed themselves to the Lord Jesus. It has been pointed out that behind the image of Diana there was an inner shrine where men could deposit their riches for safekeeping. One writer has described it as the 'Bank of England' of the ancient world. So they had abandoned their pagan way of life; they had done so at great cost to themselves and had looked to the true treasures hidden with God in Christ. Perhaps Paul had these things in mind when he took his leave of the elders of the Ephesian ecclesia:

> "And now, brethren, I commend you to God, and to the word of his grace, which is able to build you up, and to give you an inheritance among all them which are sanctified." (Acts 20:32)

The word translated "commend" means literally, 'to commit, to deposit something on trust'; hence, 'to protect or guard'. So they themselves, a peculiar treasure unto God, had been committed to His care and their eternal future was secure, for their lives were "hid with Christ in God" (Colossians 3:3).

Purity of doctrine

Paul had come to know the ecclesia at Ephesus very well. As he took his leave of the elders of the ecclesia, he reminded them of the time he had spent among them. For three years (Acts 20:31) he had earnestly given them warning of the danger in which they stood from false teachers:

> "For I know this, that after my departing shall grievous wolves enter in among you, not sparing the flock. Also of your own selves shall men arise, speaking perverse things, to draw away disciples after them." (verses 29,30)

In this respect the believers at Ephesus proved equal to the challenge. As the words of the apostle were fulfilled and the purity of the Faith they held was threatened by men of perverse minds, they held fast to the teachings that had been delivered unto them. When in the letters to the seven ecclesias of Asia the Lord Jesus spoke to them, he commended their steadfastness in combating those who would have undermined the truth of the Gospel:

> "I know thy works, and thy labour, and thy patience, and how thou canst not bear them that are evil: and thou hast tried them which say they are apostles, and are not, and hast found them liars: and hast borne, and hast patience, and for my name's sake hast laboured, and hast not fainted." (Revelation 2:2,3)

No impurity had been condoned; there had been no complicity in the evil things of Ephesus. The ecclesia had been guarded against the intrusion of wicked and unholy men. They had been careful about doctrine and had shown discernment and sound judgement in the face of false teachers.

In love

Love is the only environment in which the Truth can prosper. It must be a genuine and continuing love, and for all their success in holding fast to sound doctrine

161

they had failed to maintain that love which they had known at the beginning of their walk to the kingdom. The Lord Jesus said of them:

"Nevertheless I have somewhat against thee, because thou hast left thy first love." (Revelation 2:4)

Again, it would appear that in the three years he had spent among them Paul had come to know their weaknesses as well as their strengths.

In the epistle that he addressed to them there is a remarkable emphasis upon the importance of everything being done in love. Thus:

"That we should be holy and without blame before him *in love*." (1:4)

"That ye being rooted and grounded *in love*." (3:17)

"Forbearing one another *in love*." (4:2)

"But speaking the truth *in love* ..." (4:15)

"Maketh increase of the body unto the edifying of itself *in love*." (4:16)

"And walk *in love*, as Christ also has loved us ..." (5:2)

"Grace be with all them *that love* our Lord Jesus Christ with incorruption." (6:24, with AV margin)

What the Lord Jesus meant by their "first love" is perhaps illustrated by the words of Jeremiah:

"Thus saith the LORD; I remember thee, the kindness of thy youth, the love of thine espousals, when thou wentest after me in the wilderness, in a land that was not sown." (Jeremiah 2:2)

Strong's Concordance gives "bridehood" for the word "espousals", and we can appreciate the implication of the figure from human experience. What we might term as romantic love, the love of the honeymoon period, could mislead us a little. Surely no one lives in that sense of excitement and elation perpetually. Marriage is a commitment made between a man and a woman and that state of euphoria that might exist at the first gradually gives way to a fuller, deeper and more satisfying love that is able to remain steadfast in the face of all the trials and difficulties that the vicissitudes of life might bring.

It is surely significant that it is in his epistle to the Ephesians that the apostle uses the marriage bond, that most radiant of all illustrations, to describe the relationship that exists between the Lord Jesus and his Ecclesia (5:22-33).

To the Ephesians the Lord said, "I know thy works, and thy labour, and thy patience" (Revelation 2:2). In writing to the Thessalonians Paul said, "remembering without ceasing your work of faith, and labour of love, and patience of hope in our Lord Jesus Christ" (1 Thessalonians 1:3).

Herein lies the secret. There had been what we might call an inward backsliding. Outwardly, all their good works were manifest, but within, the springs of action by which their works should have been motivated, that steadfast love which should have maintained their relationship with the Lord Jesus, had gradually been eroded. Now their works were performed by habit and routine rather than conviction and the consequence was inevitable: their light would go out; the Lord would remove their lightstand out of its place.

Conclusion

There is much that we can learn from the Apostle Paul's relationship with the ecclesia at Ephesus. Their initial enthusiasm and willingness to suffer financial loss for the sake of the Gospel is an exhortation to us to be prepared to sacrifice this world's goods for the sake of the Lord Jesus. We too need to remember that the spiritual riches that can be ours in him will more than compensate us for any loss that we suffer.

We have a similar responsibility to maintain the purity of the faith and to reject the teaching of any that might be of a perverse mind. Above all, we must strive to maintain our love for the Lord Jesus, knowing that this is the only way in which our good works will continue, for "he that endureth to the end shall be saved" (Matthew 10:22).

163

30

CONCORDANCES

THERE can be no doubt that concordances are a most valuable tool in the study of God's word. They give English readers an insight into the meaning and usage of the original Hebrew and Greek words that would otherwise be denied them. Two concordances in particular have been used extensively within the Christadelphian community: *Young's Analytical* and *Strong's Exhaustive* concordances. Forty to fifty years ago Young's was by far the more popular but since the numerical coding in Strong's has been extended to *Gesenius' Hebrew Lexicon* and *Grimm Thayer's Greek Lexicon*, together with other works of reference, the balance has swung towards Strong's – to such an extent that one rarely hears a reference to Young's these days.

A cautionary note

While acknowledging the value of these works we feel it appropriate to sound a cautionary note. Concordances are not infallible and in interpreting the meaning of Hebrew and Greek words the compilers do not always shed themselves of their own doctrinal bias.

For instance, some time ago we saw a study paper encouraging young people, both baptized and unbaptized, to look up the meaning of various Greek words in *Strong's Concordance*. Among them was the word "grace" of which Strong says:

> "Graciousness ... of manner or act ... especially the divine influence upon the heart, and its reflection in the life ..."

This is not simply an attempt to give the meaning of the word but a doctrinal statement. The basic meaning of the Greek word *charis* is an unmerited gift and we remember that we were taught that grace was the unmerited favour of God. While acknowledging the varied shades of meaning that the Greek word has, we still believe that our Christadelphian definition adequately sums up the primary meaning of the word – although this is also, admittedly, a doctrinal statement. While we look in vain for this definition in *Strong's Concordance,* we find it reflected in Thayer's more extensive comments on the word.

What is particularly interesting is the following from the Publisher's Introduction to *Thayer's Lexicon*:

"A word of caution is necessary. Thayer was a Unitarian, and the errors of this sect occasionally come through in the explanatory notes. The reader should be alert for both subtle and blatant denials of such doctrines as the Trinity (Thayer regarded Christ as a mere man and the Holy Spirit as an impersonal force emanating from God), the inherent and total depravity of fallen human nature, the eternal punishment of the wicked and Bible inerrancy."

These words are written in a context commending the value of Strong's work, so presumably he could be relied upon to give proper emphasis to those doctrines that Thayer denied. Hence Strong says:

"Gehenna – used (fig.) as a name for the place (or state) of everlasting punishment."

We would not, for instance, share the views of Thayer on the Lord Jesus Christ or the inspiration of scripture, but the warning given is interesting for we need to be equally cautious of the Calvinistic views of Strong.

This is not written to discourage the use of these works of reference. Rather we seek to encourage a healthy scepticism, particularly where key doctrinal issues are involved. If possible, compare different works of reference as this will produce a more balanced view and, above all things, remember that these are the works of men and that consequently they lack the authority of the word of God.

31

"CHRIST DIED FOR US"

AS a community it has been a cornerstone of our belief concerning the sacrifice of the Lord Jesus Christ that he did not die as a substitute for us, but as our representative. This understanding arises out of the principles involved in the atonement. The Apostle Paul wrote:

> "But God commendeth his love toward us, in that, while we were yet sinners, Christ died for us."
>
> (Romans 5:8)

The Greek preposition *huper*, rendered "for", means 'on behalf of' (see *Vine's Expository Dictionary* and *Thayer's Greek-English Lexicon*). It is used consistently of the sacrifice of the Lord Jesus Christ (see Luke 22:19; John 6:51; 10:15; 15:13; Romans 14:15; 1 Corinthians 15:3; 2 Corinthians 5:21; Galatians 1:4 etc.). In contrast, the Greek preposition *anti*, which means 'instead of' and which could be construed as implying a substitutionary factor in the Lord's sacrifice, is used only twice in relation to it in the New Testament. These two instances are in fact parallel passages (Matthew 20:28 and Mark 10:45) and could therefore be regarded as a single instance:

> "For even the Son of Man came not to be ministered unto, but to minister, and to give his life a ransom for many." (Mark 10:45)

The principle of representation

It has been pointed out that the metaphor used requires this preposition to set the ransom against the ransomed, and the proper understanding of the passage lies in the Old Testament teaching on redemption that we cannot now develop. We believe nevertheless, that the principle of representation is clearly set forth in the Old Testament scriptures in a manner that helps us to appreciate the nature of the Lord's sacrifice. We refer to the constitution of the nation of Israel, of whom God said: "Ye shall be unto me a kingdom of priests and an holy nation" (Exodus 19:6).

In token of this truth and the fact that all the nation belonged to God, it was written, "All the firstborn are mine" (Numbers 3:13). The firstborn were representative of the whole nation. Yet in the very nature of things the firstborn could not minister before God and the Levites were taken to perform this function:

> "And thou shalt bring the Levites before the tabernacle of the congregation: and thou shalt gather the whole assembly of the children of Israel together: and thou shalt bring the Levites before the LORD: and the children of Israel shall put their hands upon the Levites: and Aaron shall offer the Levites before the LORD for an offering of the children of Israel, that they may execute the service of the LORD."
>
> (Numbers 8:9-11)

In like manner the Levites in their entirety could not perform the special functions of the priesthood. For this purpose the sons of Aaron were chosen and they alone could minister in the holy place:

> "Therefore thou and thy sons with thee shall keep your priest's office for every thing of the altar, and within the vail; and ye shall serve: I have given your priest's office unto you as a service of gift: and the stranger that cometh nigh shall be put to death."
>
> (18:7)

This principle of representation reached its climax in the office of the high priest, for only he could enter into the Most Holy Place, into the very presence of God Himself.

Israel were a priestly dynasty and everything that ideally they should have been, met and was manifest in the office of the high priest. He represented the nation of Israel as a whole and when on the Day of Atonement he entered the Most Holy Place, it was as if all Israel went with him.

There are, of course, deeper implications to this priestly hierarchy than we have outlined, but the principle of representation can be clearly seen. The people, the firstborn, the Levites, the priests, all finally converge in the person of the high priest.

Crucified with Christ

Thus it was with the sacrifice of the Lord Jesus Christ. We all deserve to die because of our sin. We all merit that death on the cross. But, if we might so express it, that would have been a physical impossibility. Nevertheless in the Lord Jesus, God has graciously given us a representation of the truth of the matter in one who was a sinless bearer of our nature. If we believe in the reality of that which the cross represents and associate ourselves with it through baptism, then symbolically we are crucified with Christ. We look at Christ crucified and we see ourselves represented in him. This is only possible because he shared our nature, and in every sense inherited the condemnation that is ours in Adam. In this way he died for us.

Let us never forget, however, that this principle of representation goes beyond the Lord's death on the cross. When the high priest entered the Most Holy Place he did so on behalf of all Israel. So the Lord Jesus has done for us:

"Having therefore, brethren, boldness to enter into the holiest by the blood of Jesus, by a new and living way, which he hath consecrated for us, through the veil, that is to say, his flesh; and having an high priest over the house of God; let us draw near with a true heart in full assurance of faith." (Hebrews 10:19-22)

Because we have been "united with him" (Romans 6:5, RV) by baptism we have, as it were, been carried 'in him' into the very presence of God. It is because we are represented by him there that we are able to offer acceptable worship to our Heavenly Father. It is

168

because our works are offered to God through him that He is pleased to accept them:

"By him therefore let us offer the sacrifice of praise to God continually, that is, the fruit of our lips giving thanks to his name. But to do good and communicate forget not: for with such sacrifices God is well pleased." (Hebrews 13:15,16)

32

RIGHTEOUS LOT

IF it were not for the Apostle Peter's reference to Lot in his second epistle, it is doubtful whether many of us would have come to the conclusion that he was a righteous man from whose example we can learn valuable lessons. The record in Genesis might have left us with the impression that he was a foolish man who was only saved from the destruction that fell upon Sodom through the intercession of Abraham (Genesis 18:23-33).

Certainly he did not show spiritual discernment in the choice that he made to live in Sodom, and though delivered by God he lost his wife and other members of his family in the catastrophe that overtook the city (Genesis 19:14).

Nevertheless, he travelled with Abraham from Haran to the land of Canaan and we can only conclude that he knew something of the promises that God had made to his father's brother and was anxious to be associated with him.

Abraham and Lot

We need to remember that Lot lived in the shadow of one of the greatest men who has ever lived and the contrast between their respective outlooks is clearly seen in Genesis chapter 13. The record tells us that a dissension arose between the herdmen of Abraham and those of Lot because they had both increased their flocks and herds substantially and the land was not able to bear them both. In this situation the customs of the day dictated that Lot should have deferred to Abraham as he was the elder. Moreover, it was to Abraham that God had promised the land and consequently we might expect Lot to have recognised that the right of choice lay with his uncle and not with him. Abraham, however, anxious that there should be no strife between them, showed a magnanimous spirit and generously gave to Lot the choice of where he would prefer to live and to graze his sheep and cattle (verses 5-9).

What follows emphasises the distinction between the two men. Lot "lifted up his eyes, and beheld all the plain of Jordan". It was an attractive proposition and Lot had no hesitation in choosing this tract of land for himself, for it was "even as the garden of the LORD" (verses 10,11). The result was that whereas Abraham dwelt in the land of Canaan, Lot dwelt in the cities of the plain and pitched his tent towards Sodom (verse 12).

There can be no doubt that in making his decision Lot lacked the spiritual perception that would have enabled him to see the dangers that living in this particular area posed, for "the men of Sodom were wicked and sinners before the LORD exceedingly" (verse 13).

The name 'Lot' is derived from the Hebrew word for 'veil' (*Strong's Concordance*) and it has been suggested that literally it means, 'the man with a veil over his eyes'. This would certainly have been true of Lot on this occasion for he saw only the material benefit and was blind to the peril in which he was putting himself and his family. There is of course a warning for us in these events, for we must learn to show discretion in life in the choices that we make. The world and what it has to offer can appear very appealing and perhaps in material terms we can see great advantages in pursuing a particular course of action.

However, spiritual discernment should always prevail in any decisions we make in life, and we should always be careful to ensure that unlike Lot we do not have a veil over our eyes in comparing what the world has to offer with our spiritual well-being.

171

Significantly, after Lot had departed, a similar form of words to Lot's actions in making his choice is used by God to assure Abraham of His faithfulness to His promises:

> "Lift up now thine eyes, and look from the place where thou art northward, and southward, and eastward, and westward: for all the land which thou seest, to thee will I give it, and to thy seed for ever ... Arise, walk through the land in the length of it and in the breadth of it; for I will give it unto thee."

(verses 14-17)

Peter's testimony

Nevertheless, although he acted foolishly on this occasion, Lot was essentially a righteous man and we have the testimony of Peter to confirm this:

> "And turning the cities of Sodom and Gomorrha into ashes condemned them with an overthrow, making them an ensample unto those that after should live ungodly; and delivered just Lot, vexed with the filthy conversation of the wicked: (for that righteous man dwelling among them, in seeing and hearing, vexed his righteous soul from day to day with their unlawful deeds)."   (2 Peter 2:6-8)

Interestingly, two different Greek words have been translated "vex". The first means, 'to wear down, to harass' (Strong) and suggests that Lot did not just suffer in his heart and mind, but also by his witnessing against them was subject to hostility and animosity. It is elsewhere translated as "oppress". This is actually supported by the record in Genesis 19 which describes the reaction of the Sodomites to Lot when he withstood them before the door of his house:

> "And they said, Stand back. And they said again, This one fellow came in to sojourn, and he will needs be a judge (literally, he is always judging)." (verse 9)

In effect they said, 'You are not one of us, you don't live like us. You don't belong here and you are always judging and criticising our way of life'.

The second word translated "vexed" means literally 'to torture', and it aptly describes the inner torment and anguish that Lot experienced in seeing the wickedness of their deeds and hearing the foulness of their language. This is something that Lot endured from day to day. It was a continuing experience and we might wonder why he remained among them. Surely the answer is that although Lot himself was anxious to leave, he had family who were happy to remain there – a wife, daughters and sons-in-law. Thus Lot must have been torn between the anguish of staying amongst these lawless people and leaving those who were near and dear to him, and who appear to have become an integral part of the city's social life. The solution was not one that he would have chosen for himself, but "the Lord knoweth how to deliver the godly out of temptations" (2 Peter 2:9), and though Lot and two of his daughters were delivered, he lost the remainder of his family.

Such are the situations in which the followers of the Lord Jesus can, on occasions, find themselves. By foolish choices they can create spiritual dilemmas for themselves, and though God provides a way of escape it might involve great loss and unhappiness in their personal circumstances.

The sin of Sodom

Genesis describes the dreadful wickedness of the Sodomites, and so does Peter in his second epistle. However, other references emphasise their preoccupation with the everyday things of life to the exclusion of God. Thus the prophet Ezekiel, in comparing the wickedness of Jerusalem with that of Sodom, writes:

> "Behold, this was the iniquity of thy sister Sodom; pride, fullness of bread, and prosperous ease was in her and in her daughters; neither did she strengthen the hand of the poor and needy." (Ezekiel 16:49, RV)

Similarly the Lord Jesus testified:

"Likewise also as it was in the days of Lot; they did eat, they drank, they bought, they sold, they planted, they builded; but the same day that Lot went out of Sodom it rained fire and brimstone from heaven, and destroyed them all. Even thus shall it be in the day when the Son of man is revealed. In that day, he which shall be upon the housetop, and his stuff in the house, let him not come down to take it away: and he that is in the field, let him likewise not return back. Remember Lot's wife." (Luke 17:28-32)

The lesson is that when men leave God out of their lives and become obsessed with the material things of life, they create the environment in which the thinking of the flesh dominates and the grosser sins of which Sodom was guilty are able to flourish.

This, of course, is particularly true of the society in which most of us live today, and the risk of being anxious for the things of this life to the detriment to seeking first the kingdom of God is an ever present danger.

Notice also the context in which the Lord Jesus exhorts us to remember Lot's wife. The man on the housetop and the man in the field both went back for their stuff. Is the Lord Jesus telling us that Lot's wife did not simply look back but turned back, because that was where her heart was?

Grieved because of the wicked

Lot's reaction to the wickedness of Sodom stands as an exhortation to us in this godless world in which we live. Here is a yardstick to measure our own reactions to the gross wickedness that surrounds us. Are we indifferent to it, having become accustomed to the way in which men behave, or do we feel a sense of grief and anguish because of the way in which men abuse God's goodness and ignore His moral precepts? Just how we should feel about human sin and immoral behaviour is made clear in the pages of scripture.

Having described the abominations that were practised in secret (chapter 8), the prophet Ezekiel tells how he saw a man with an inkhorn who was commanded:

"Go through the midst of the city, through the midst of Jerusalem, and set a mark upon the foreheads of the men that sigh and that cry for all the abominations that be done in the midst thereof."

(Ezekiel 9:4)

We cannot be indifferent to sin for we remember it was written of the Lord Jesus that he loved righteousness and hated iniquity. Although written by David, the words of Psalm 119 surely reflect the spirit of the Lord Jesus who lived amongst sinners and more than any other must have grieved because of the waywardness of men:

"Horror hath taken hold upon me because of the wicked that forsake thy law." (verse 53)

"Rivers of waters run down mine eyes, because they keep not thy law." (verse 136)

"I beheld the transgressors, and was grieved; because they kept not thy word." (verse 158)

Herein is the spirit of all those who love God's word and who seek to follow His precepts. Herein is a reflection of the example of Lot who vexed his righteous soul from day to day with the unlawful deeds of the Sodomites.

33

LESSONS FROM ESTHER

THE Book of Esther stands almost alone in scripture in as much that God is not mentioned once in its pages. Readers might be aware of Bullinger's suggestion that the name of God can be found in the Hebrew text in the form of an anagram, but this is not something that the present writer feels qualified to comment on. The only reference that can be considered as referring to the work of God is found in chapter 4 – the words of Mordecai to Esther when he heard of the king's commandment that all the Jews should be killed:

> "For if thou altogether holdest thy peace at this time, then shall there enlargement and deliverance arise to the Jews from another place ... and who knoweth whether thou art come to the kingdom for such a time as this?"   (verse 14)

Nevertheless these words suggest a thread of thought that, together with Bullinger's suggestion, opens up a remarkable emphasis upon the providential hand of God at work in the affairs of His people, unseen and unknown to those who thought to do them harm.

The providence of God

It is easy to miss the time periods mentioned in the book. It was in the third year of his reign that Ahasuerus held the feast which resulted in Vashti being removed from her position as queen (1:3). The process that led to Esther being chosen as a replacement did not occur immediately, but some four years later in the seventh year of his reign (2:16); and the confrontation between Mordecai and Haman did not take place for

176

another four years or so after Esther had become queen, in the twelfth year of the king's reign (3:7).

Into this setting we have to place the events recorded. Eight years before the crisis that the book describes occurred, God had begun to make preparations for the impending emergency. We have a stubborn woman who, for reasons that are not completely clear, refused to comply with her husband's wishes, although almost certainly it was his intention that she should display herself in an immodest manner before the assembled princes. At the instigation of his chamberlains Vashti was removed from her royal status and although the king seems to have relented (2:1), his servants prevailed upon him to search the kingdom for a suitable replacement. This led to Esther finding favour above all the others chosen and she was eventually made queen instead of Vashti. Thus the scene was set for the events that were yet to transpire.

But God's hand was at work in other ways. Mordecai sat in the king's gate, for he had evidently risen to a position of some eminence. While carrying out his duties he learned that two of the king's chamberlains were plotting to do the king harm. He reported this matter to Esther who in turn told the necessary authorities, and the matter was recorded in the chronicles of the king in the name of Mordecai (2:21-23). No further action was taken at that time, and it would appear from the timescales mentioned above that it must have occurred shortly after the establishment of Esther as queen and therefore some three to four years before Haman became a threat, not only to Mordecai but to all the Jews.

It was in the midst of this crisis that the king experienced a sleepless night. Had he eaten too much? Was he suffering from indigestion? It could be any one of a number of trivial causes, but whereas the modern advice is to count sheep, he called for the record of the chronicles of the kingdom to be read to him (6:1). The result was that the reports of four years previously concerning Mordecai and the treacherous chamberlains were read to the king and he was moved to ask what reward had been given to the man who had rendered this service. It is truly remarkable that in all the events recorded the hand of God is clearly seen. For Mordecai and Esther and all the people of the Jews it was a time of crisis. Haman's determination to destroy them left them bereft of hope; it seemed, humanly speaking, that there was no way out from the emergency they faced. Nevertheless, the record in the Book of Esther clearly establishes that though His servants might go through times of crisis and anxiety this is not so with God, for He had prepared the way and under His providential hand the means of deliverance had been arranged before the crisis itself had arisen.

What irony that Haman, believing that he alone was the one whom the king would honour, should speak the words that would ultimately lead to his own downfall (6:4-11). There is of course a great lesson here for us in our lives, for we too can pass through times of crisis and emergency. The Proverb says:

"In all thy ways acknowledge him, and he shall make straight thy paths." (Proverbs 3:6, RV margin)

The Hebrew is identical with the words of the prophet Isaiah who declared:

"The voice of him that crieth in the wilderness, Prepare ye the way of the LORD, make straight in the desert a highway for our God." (40:3)

The figure behind these words is the manner in which a king or person of great importance, in making a journey, would send messengers before him to make the way straight by the removal of any obstructions that would impede his journey. So if we acknowledge God in all our ways and recognise His providential hand, we can be assured that whatever spiritual dilemma we might find ourselves in, our God will have gone before and prepared the way – removing, if necessary, any impediment or stumblingblock that might hinder our walk to His kingdom. In this respect

God treats us as men would have treated royalty and we can rejoice in the knowledge that it is His good pleasure to give us the kingdom (Luke 12:32).

Mordecai the Jew

The misgivings that some have with the Book of Esther do not just rest on the absence of any clear reference to the God of Israel. The character of Mordecai has also come under critical scrutiny. He has been described as a political opportunist and some have suggested that it was his attitude towards Haman that provoked the crisis. It is asserted that he acted throughout in a high-handed and vengeful manner, being moved by self-interest rather than any spiritual motive.

It should be noted, however, that Haman's quarrel was not just with Mordecai but with all the Jews in the kingdom, for he persuaded the king to issue a decree that they should all be delivered into his hands because of the diversity of their laws and their manner of living (Esther 3:6,8-13). He is declared to be "the Jews' enemy" and clearly there is far more to the events recorded than those of a critical disposition have appreciated.

It is interesting to note the manner in which the two leading characters are introduced to us, for it would appear that there is a deliberate emphasis that directs our attention to a particular event in Old Testament history.

Mordecai is described as "the son of Jair, the son of Shimei, the son of Kish, a Benjamite" (2:5). Whether or not the reference is to Kish the father of Saul, the first king of Israel to whom Mordecai could trace his genealogy, the link with Saul appears to be evident, for Shimei, who cursed David, was also of the house of Saul (2 Samuel 16:5). Furthermore, it was said of Saul that "from his shoulders and upward he was higher than any of the people" (1 Samuel 9:2; 10:23). There is a play on Saul's physical presence when he sinned in the matter of the Amalekites for Samuel said to him, "When thou wast little in thine own sight, wast thou not made head of the tribes of Israel?" (15:17). Significantly, *Kitto's*

Encyclopaedia of Bible Knowledge points out that among the suggestions for the meaning of Mordecai's name is one claiming that it is of Persian origin, meaning 'little man', an obvious contrast with King Saul. Interestingly, the name that Saul of Tarsus took for himself was 'Paul' which, *Strong's Concordance* tells us, means 'little'.

Similarly the information concerning Haman directs us back to the historical record in 1 Samuel 15. He is described as the Agagite (Esther 3:1). Whether he had a direct connection with the Agag slain by Samuel, or had taken the name because of his admiration for the man, we are clearly intended to understand that he was an Amalekite. He belonged to a race that were the great enemies of God's people. God had said they were to blot out the remembrance of them from under heaven (Deuteronomy 25:17-19); and again, "the LORD will have war with Amalek from generation to generation" (Exodus 17:16).

Herein lies the reason for Mordecai's refusal to prostrate himself before Haman. In a sense there was a re-enactment of Saul's encounter with Agag. Mordecai was determined that he would not show honour and respect to an Amalekite who gloried in the name of that ancient king Agag. Mordecai was put under great pressure for his contemporaries, noting his behaviour, reported his actions to Haman. Notice that his defence was, "I am a Jew" (Esther 3:4). He was determined to maintain his identity as one of the distinctive people of God. He would not compromise himself but would remain faithful to Israel's God, remembering the failure of Saul so long before when confronted by the Amalekites. In this respect he was representative of the Jews as a whole (verse 8), and their behaviour stands as an example to us of how by our manner of life we should retain our identity as the people of God, and witness for Him before those amongst whom we live.

The connection with Saul and Agag does not end here, for Samuel had commanded Saul that not only was he to destroy the people but "ox and sheep, camel and ass" (1 Samuel 15:3). The people, however, provoked God's anger for they took of the spoil, and this also is reflected in the events recorded in the book of Esther. Haman having received his just deserts, the king commanded that not only should the Jews be permitted to destroy those who sought to harm them, but also they were allowed "to take the spoil of them for a prey" (Esther 8:11).

However, unlike Israel in the days of Saul, surely under the instruction of Mordecai, the record tells us that "on the spoil laid they not their hand" (9:10,15,16). They were determined to behave in a manner that reflected the standards God had established in respect of the Amalekites. Again the lesson is there for us. In our endeavours to maintain our integrity and identity we must be diligent not to seek to take the spoil. Amalek stands for the carnal mind, the flesh and all that it delights in. How careful we must be not to gather to ourselves the things that the world has to offer. We must remember that we "cannot serve God and mammon" (Matthew 6:24).

Perhaps the most remarkable thing of all is that by the manner in which Mordecai and the Jews conducted themselves, they made such an impression on those amongst whom they lived that "many of the people of the land became Jews; for the fear of the Jews fell upon them" (Esther 8:17; 9:27). Such was the power of their witness that people were won for the God of Israel. We too need to witness in word and by the manner of our living, that we also might make an impression on those amongst whom we live and, by God's grace, win some for the Lord Jesus Christ.

Conclusion

The difficulties that some find in the Book of Esther must therefore be set against the obvious manner in which the conflict between Mordecai, the Jew, and Haman, the Amalekite, runs through the record with its echo of the historical events of 1 Samuel 15. The lessons of the book are powerful for they speak to us of the providential hand of God which is continually working on our behalf; and of the need for us, in the confidence this should produce, to witness in word and deed to the greatness of our calling that others might be brought to a knowledge of saving truth.

"But sanctify the Lord God in your hearts: and be ready always to give an answer to every man that asketh you a reason of the hope that is in you with meekness and fear." (1 Peter 3:15)

34

ANOTHER LOOK AT JUDAS ISCARIOT

IT was at the beginning of the last year of his ministry that we have the first indication that the identity of the one who should betray him was known to the Lord Jesus (John 6:64-71). Of course the Gospel writers, in listing the names of the apostles, had indicated that Judas Iscariot was the traitor, but this was with the benefit of hindsight (Matthew 10:4; Mark 3:19; Luke 6:16). John's Gospel says:

"But there are some of you that believe not. For Jesus knew from the beginning who they were that believed not, and who should betray him."   (6:64)

"Jesus knew from the beginning ..."

There is a difficulty here, for was it the intention of John to impress upon us that when the Lord chose Judas Iscariot he already knew that he would betray him and consequently selected him for that very purpose? If such be the case it presents us with a very real moral dilemma, for it becomes hard to escape the conclusion that Judas was thus predestined to condemnation and that he was placed in a situation in which he had no option but to play out his predetermined part. That the Lord Jesus knew that one of the twelve would betray him is beyond question, for Old Testament prophecy would have led him to that conclusion from the very beginning (Psalm 41:9; 55:12-14). It must surely be true, however, that although God knows the ultimate destiny of every man, He calls no one merely to consign him to eternal oblivion. God is longsuffering, "not willing that any should perish, but that all should come to repentance" (2 Peter 3:9). Thus when the Lord "ordained twelve that they should be

183

with him" (Mark 3:14), he selected men of potential, who possessed those qualities and abilities that made it possible for them to be transformed into everything that he desired them to be. At this juncture that was as true of Judas Iscariot as of the other disciples.

What then did John mean when he wrote that the Lord Jesus knew from the beginning who should betray him? Several writers point out that "from the beginning" is a relative term that must be interpreted strictly in context (*Thayer's Greek-English Lexicon* – "in a relative sense, the beginning of the thing spoken of").

The context in John 6 describes how, after the feeding of the five thousand, the multitude recognised in the miracle a Messianic act and would have taken the Lord Jesus by force to make him a king. He restrained them in their enthusiasm, and the following day delivered his discourse on the bread of life that led many to say:

"This is an hard saying; who can hear it? When Jesus knew in himself that his disciples murmured at it, he saith unto them, Doth this offend you?"

(John 6:60,61)

In other words, the Lord Jesus, because he knew what was in man, from the very first signs of unbelief in those who would go back and walk no more with him (verse 66), became aware of their scepticism and incredulity. He knew from the beginning, that is from their earliest moment of doubt, how they would eventually react.

This of course in no way removed their personal responsibility for their actions. Was it at this juncture that the seeds of distrust were sown into the mind of Judas and recognised by the Lord Jesus? His heart was with those who went back, but he chose to remain with the Lord and took the first step that was to lead him, in spite of the Lord's gentle and fervent entreaties, to play the part of which the prophetic word had spoken. It was nevertheless his choice; at the point of betrayal Luke tells us that "he went his way, and communed with the chief priests and captains" (22:4). It was by his own deliberate intent that he chose this path.

184

"That they should be with him"

Mark records that the Lord Jesus "ordained twelve, that they should be with him" (3:14). In the remainder of the chapter we have a description of how the Lord establishes a new family relationship with those whom he had called – based, not on natural ties, but on spiritual values (verse 19; see AV margin and verses 31-35). Amongst them was Judas Iscariot.

Like the others he was called to great things. His association with the Lord Jesus and the work entrusted to his hand could have made him; instead it broke him. He could have reached the heights; instead he plumbed the depths. He was given great privilege because of the potential that he showed and to the very last the Lord gave him every opportunity to turn from his chosen path. At the commencement of the final week of his ministry, the Lord gave the twelve an assurance that "in the regeneration when the Son of man shall sit in the throne of his glory, ye also shall sit upon twelve thrones, judging the twelve tribes of Israel" (Matthew 19:28). Even at this late juncture these words could have been as true for Judas as the other disciples. But the Lord knew his heart, and surely the words that followed were a solemn warning to this man who was already involved with the rulers of the people in their plot to kill the Lord Jesus: "But many that are first shall be last; and the last shall be first" (verse 30). As we shall see, the parable that follows would seem to confirm this conclusion.

Judas lacked none of the benefits enjoyed by the other disciples. He listened to all the gracious words that proceeded out of the mouth of the Lord Jesus; he saw, with the others, the miracles that he performed. He was there when the Lord raised the widow of Nain's son; when he walked on the water and stilled the storm; when he fed the five thousand and the four thousand; he saw Lazarus raised from the dead. He was a witness to all these wonderful works and when the Lord sent forth the twelve to the lost sheep of the house of Israel, he played a full part in their ministry.

Of those whom he had chosen the Lord said, "Ye are they which have continued with me in my temptations" (Luke 22:28). Although Judas at this time had left to complete his negotiations with the rulers of the people, the words must have been true of him also during the three-and-a-half years of the ministry. This, surely, is evident from the manner in which the Lord took the twelve to himself again during the last year of his ministry:

> "And (Jesus) took again the twelve, and began to tell them what things should happen unto him."
>
> (Mark 10:32)

Strong's Concordance says of the word "took", that it means "to receive near, i.e., to associate with oneself (in any familiar or intimate act or relation)". Such was the warmth and closeness of the Lord's relationship with the disciples including, of course, Judas Iscariot.

"Mine own familiar friend"

A consideration of two of the psalms most closely associated with the treachery of Judas gives us an insight into the relationship he had with the Lord Jesus that is perhaps not always appreciated.

> "Yea, mine own familiar friend, in whom I trusted, which did eat of my bread, hath lifted up his heel against me." (Psalm 41:9)

That the words have an application to Judas is beyond doubt, for the Lord Jesus quotes them in this connection (John 13:18). The occasion was the last night of his mortal life, and the Lord's omission of the words "in whom I trusted" is understandable as he knew that Judas would shortly leave to conclude his act of treachery. Nevertheless, the words of the psalm must be true for there was a time in the early days of the ministry when there was a closeness of identity, a bond of trust. He was "the man of my peace" (Psalm 41:9, AV margin) and the words suggest the sense of rapport

186

that existed between them in those early days. There is a connection with the second of these psalms, for again the AV margin helps us in rendering the words "lifted up his heel" as "magnified his heel" – a fact emphasised in Psalm 55:

"For it was not an enemy that reproached me; then I could have borne it; neither was it he that hated me that did magnify himself against me; then I could have hid myself from him: but it was thou, a man mine equal, my guide, and mine acquaintance. We took sweet counsel together, and walked into the house of God in company."   (verses 12-14)

Again there is the suggestion of a closeness of identity, an affinity, a meeting of minds.

Was there in some respects a special relationship? Did Judas have a greater knowledge than the others? Did he, at first, show more understanding of the Lord's teaching? Perhaps he was more sophisticated, a better educated man than the others. Whether or not this is so, he certainly did not come to understand the Lord in the manner in which the others developed their relationship. This is made clear by their individual response to the Lord's words that one of them would betray him (Matthew 26:21-25). Shocked, appalled by the very thought, they each asked him in turn, "Lord, is it I?"; but not Judas, for he in the full knowledge of what he had already done and what he was shortly to accomplish, said not "Lord" but "Master, is it I?" The eleven, for all their bewilderment and uncertainty, were still convinced that he was the Messiah, but Judas Iscariot no longer shared that conviction.

Both Psalm 41 and 55 say of the traitor that "he magnified himself". To express it colloquially, "he made himself big". He had an inflated sense of his own importance and the Lord's failure, in his eyes, to take the necessary action to establish the kingdom was a denial of all the power and influence that Judas had hoped for when he first followed the Lord Jesus. It is surely significant that the very next verse in Psalm 55 has an obvious reference to Korah, Dathan and Abiram, who coveted the positions of Moses and Aaron as the leaders of God's people:

> "Let death seize upon them, and let them go down quick into hell: for wickedness is in their dwellings, and among them." (verse 15)

The supper at Bethany

Six days before the final Passover the Lord Jesus, with the twelve, came to Bethany where a supper was prepared for him. It was on this occasion that Mary brought a pound of ointment of spikenard and anointed the feet of Jesus, wiping them with her hair (John 12:1-3). It was an act of love and devotion that touched the heart of the Lord, for the ointment was very precious and if sold would have paid the wages of a labourer for almost a year. The reaction of the disciples, however, was different for at the instigation of Judas they complained that the ointment should have been sold and the money given to the poor (verses 4,5). John adds the pertinent comment:

> "This he said, not that he cared for the poor; but because he was a thief, and had the bag, and bare (RV, took away) what was put therein." (verse 6)

Judas Iscariot is revealed as a greedy and covetous man who was motivated by self-interest, and the incident is important for the insight it gives into the things that Judas looked for in life. The response of the Lord Jesus was:

> "Let her alone: against the day of my burying hath she kept this." (verse 7)

There can be little doubt that as the last Passover approached there had been an air of melancholy that had encompassed both the Lord and the disciples. He had spoken repeatedly about his impending death at Jerusalem, and his bearing and demeanour throughout this time must have left his disciples bewildered and confused. Mary, although not fully understanding the true nature of the events that were shortly to transpire, had appreciated the meaning of his words and she had kept the ointment against such a day. She was not alone, however, in appreciating that the Lord was talking of his imminent death, for Judas also had grasped the significance of his words, and for him it was the catalyst that would bring his betrayal to a speedy conclusion. After all, he had given up everything for this man. He had followed him and cultivated his friendship in the conviction that he was the Messiah who would reward him with a position of honour and power when the kingdom was established – and now all he could talk of was dying.

Even if, as some suggest, he was trying to put the Lord Jesus into a situation that would compel him to reveal himself as king, the fact remains that he was motivated not by a love of the Lord but by self-interest and personal ambition.

Thus it was that after he had washed the disciples' feet (John 13), the Lord precipitated the situation, showing that he knew of Judas' treachery and urging him to do that which he had determined more quickly (verses 18-30). John concludes this section of his record with the words: "He then having received the sop went immediately out: and it was night." John is of course recording accurately the time of day, but the phrase is also pregnant with spiritual significance. Judas could not remain in the presence of the Lord Jesus, in the light that shone into his heart and revealed him for what he was. He was of the night, and he went out into that gathering darkness that was to envelop him and lay hold on him forever.

Some final reflections

We referred earlier to the promise of the Lord Jesus that his disciples should sit on twelve thrones judging the twelve tribes of Israel, and the ominous words of warning that followed:

"Many that are first shall be last; and the last shall be first." (Matthew 19:27-30)

189

This warning was illustrated by the parable of the labourers in the vineyard which follows immediately. The first labourers to be hired reached an agreement with the lord of the vineyard that they should be paid a penny a day (20:2). Subsequently others were hired at the third, sixth, ninth and eleventh hours to labour in the vineyard (verses 3-6). When, however, the lord of the vineyard instructed his steward to pay the labourers, they were given "every man a penny" (verses 8,9). Those that had borne the heat and burden of the day were disgruntled and murmured, expecting that they should have received more (verses 10-12). The close of the parable is significant, for the Goodman of the house does not address them all, but "he answered one of them, and said, Friend, I do thee no wrong, didst not thou agree with me for a penny?" Was it a word of warning to Judas? Note that the concluding words of the parable are a repetition of those that closed chapter 19:

"So the last shall be first, and the first last: for many be called, but few chosen." (20:16)

Surely one of the lessons of the parable is that we cannot presume that the Lord Jesus is in any way indebted to us; we cannot react to him as though we have rights that he is obliged to fulfil. This was the problem with Judas Iscariot: he had followed out of self-interest. He considered himself entitled to the expected reward when the Lord came into his kingdom. That the parable was directed principally at Judas is suggested by the word that the Lord Jesus used in addressing the one to whom he responded – "Friend". It is characteristic of Matthew's Gospel and it means literally 'comrade'. Was this the usual way that the Lord spoke to Judas – comrade? It was certainly the way in which he addressed him at the time of his betrayal:

"Friend (comrade), wherefore art thou come?"

(26:50)

If this was indeed the familiar way in which the Lord addressed him, how significant it is that in another parable the Lord used the word, surely as a warning and an appeal:

"Friend (comrade) how camest thou in hither not having a wedding garment?"   (22:12)

Of one thing we can be certain: the Lord Jesus would have made every effort to turn this man away from that course he had determined to follow.

Perhaps the habitual way in which he is described sums up the character of the man: Judas Iscariot – Judas, man of Kerioth. It is suggested by some that the name Kerioth means literally, 'two cities'. He was a man of two cities, for although he followed the Lord Jesus desiring honour and power in God's kingdom, he was also a covetous man motivated by self-interest and he sought the things that this world had to offer. He tried to serve God and Mammon.

Perhaps the saddest fact of all is that it is written of this man, whom the Lord Jesus had chosen to be *with* him (Mark 3:14), that when the soldiers came to arrest the Lord, "Judas also, which betrayed him, stood *with* them" (John 18:5).

Such were the depths to which this man of great potential had sunk.

35

STRIKING METAPHORS IN JUDE

IN considering the character of the false teachers and warning of the danger they presented to the brethren and sisters to whom he wrote, Jude uses five dramatic figures of speech to demonstrate their true nature. They are described in verses 12 and 13 as follows:

"Spots (RV, hidden rocks) in your feasts of charity (RV, love-feasts)."

"Clouds they are without water."

"Trees whose fruit withereth."

"Raging waves of the sea."

"Wandering stars."

Epithet is added to epithet and metaphor to metaphor in some of the strongest language recorded in scripture, as Jude describes the character and destiny of these evil men who sought, deliberately, to destroy from within the ecclesias to which they belonged.

"Hidden rocks in your love-feasts"

We have reproduced the RV rendering of these words because although the English of the AV in 2 Peter and Jude is almost identical, the Greek text has two different words, *spiloi* (2 Peter 2:13) and *spilades* (Jude verse 12). *Ellicott's Commentary* sums the matter up well when it says, "Peter's word may mean either 'spots' or 'rocks' (though most commonly the former), Jude's word may mean either 'spots' or 'rocks' (although almost invariably the latter)". It concludes that in Jude, "rocks" is the safer translation. So these false brethren were like hidden rocks as they attended the love-feasts; lying undetected, on which the unwary could make shipwreck of their faith (1 Timothy 1:19).

192

The "love-feast" was the communal meal that brethren and sisters enjoyed together. From the earliest days it appears to have been associated with the Lord's Supper and to have been shared immediately before they proceeded to remember the death and resurrection of the Lord Jesus in bread and wine. It was a testimony to their fellowship in the Gospel as rich and poor sat together and shared a common meal. It was intended to be a feast of love and no doubt the feeding of the poor was one of its primary objects. The abuse to which the meal was sometimes subject is evident from Paul's first epistle to Corinth (11:17-22).

However, it was certainly not just to do with eating and drinking. It was about conversation, exchanges of views and experiences that would strengthen and encourage those that participated. Surely, here lay the danger – in the table talk of these false teachers who presented themselves as shepherds of the flock but who were in reality feeding themselves. Literally Jude says that they were 'pasturing themselves'. It is the same word that is used in a positive sense by both Peter and Paul (1 Peter 5:2; Acts 20:28). These men, however, who postured as pastors, were in reality like the shepherds of Israel condemned in Ezekiel 34, and it is this scripture that Jude must have reflected on as he wrote his epistle:

> "Woe be to the shepherds of Israel that do feed themselves! should not the shepherds feed the flocks? … My flock became a prey, and my flock became meat to every beast of the field, because there was no shepherd, neither did my shepherds search for my flock, but the shepherds fed themselves, and fed not my flock."   (Ezekiel 34:2,8)

Thus these false teachers indulged themselves in their fancies and used the flock for their own advantage. They did so "without fear" for there was no real awareness of God. They did not fear Him but behaved as though He saw not, nor heard, the manner of their living, or the selfish motives that lay behind their secret agenda.

"Clouds without water"

These are full of promise but deliver nothing. In the east the appearance of clouds held the promise of rain. It was with bitter disappointment that men would behold them carried away by the wind, leaving the ground as hard and as unrefreshed as before their appearance. So men looked to these false shepherds and realised that as clouds without rain, for all their show and ostentation, they had no spiritual refreshment to give. They themselves were "carried about by every wind of doctrine" (Ephesians 4:14).

Jude had a proverb in mind when writing these words: "Whoso boasteth himself of a false gift is like clouds and wind without rain" (Proverbs 25:14). The words of the proverb are particularly appropriate if we remember that these men claimed to speak with an authority equal to that of the apostles. They too claimed to possess the gift of the Holy Spirit. Their boast, however, was false and the evidence was to be seen in the spiritual havoc they had caused amongst the brethren and sisters upon whom they fed themselves to their own advantage. "By their fruits ye shall know them" (Matthew 7:20). Appropriately, the next metaphor develops this truth.

"Trees whose fruit withereth"

There are here echoes of the words of John the Baptist and the Lord Jesus (see Matthew 3:10; 7:16-20; Luke 13:6-9, and the enacted parable of the barren fig tree).

Literally Jude calls them "autumn trees without fruit" (RV). At the very time that men might legitimately have expected to find fruit, there was none. Instead they withered and died – indeed, they were twice dead (literally 'they have died twice'). What does Jude mean? Is it that they had died unto sin in the waters of baptism and now they have died again in returning to their former manner of life, like the dog to its vomit and the sow to its wallowing in the mire? Possibly. But we suggest that Jude is continuing this vivid and dramatic figure of the fruitless tree. It was considered dead when it bore no fruit, but it was twice dead in that when the sap dries up from the tree there is no hope of renewal. There had been no fruit unto righteousness and the result was the complete loss of their spiritual life. They were fit for nothing but to be plucked up by the roots and cast into the fire (Matthew 3:10).

This raises questions about human behaviour and God's willingness to forgive. Does there come a time when men are beyond renewal? The scriptural answer is yes. If men persist in their evil ways in the face of all attempts to show them the right way; if they harden their hearts and stiffen their necks, then a time comes when they are so set in their own way, so set in their habitual wickedness, that it is impossible for them to change. When this happens God confirms them in the choice they have made. It is not that God is unwilling to forgive, but rather that they are unwilling to be forgiven.

The principle is clearly seen in the following scriptures:

"For the invisible things of him from the creation of the world are clearly seen, being understood by the things that are made, even his eternal power and Godhead; so that they are without excuse: because that, when they knew God, they glorified him not as God, neither were thankful; but became vain in their imaginations, and their foolish heart was darkened. Professing themselves to be wise, they became fools, and changed the glory of the uncorruptible God into an image made like to corruptible man, and to birds, and fourfooted beasts, and creeping things. Wherefore God also gave them up to uncleanness through the lusts of their own hearts ... And even as they did not like to retain God in their knowledge, God gave them over to a reprobate mind, to do those things which are not convenient."

(Romans 1:20-24,28)

"And then shall that Wicked be revealed, whom the Lord shall consume with the spirit of his mouth, and shall destroy with the brightness of his coming: even him, whose coming is after the working of Satan with all power and signs and lying wonders, and with all deceivableness of unrighteousness in them that perish; because they received not the love of the truth, that they might be saved. And for this cause God shall send them strong delusion, that they should believe a lie: that they all might be damned who believed not the truth, but had pleasure in unrighteousness."   (2 Thessalonians 2:8-12)

In each of these examples, like the potter's vessel that cannot be made whole again (Jeremiah 18 and 19), they had pursued their own way with such determination that it had become impossible for them to change. Of their own choice they had refused the opportunity of forgiveness and God had confirmed the choice they made. Such are truly twice dead.

"Raging waves of the sea"

The shameless behaviour of these men is likened to the raging of the seas. Again we hear the echoes of scripture:

"Peace, peace to him that is far off, and to him that is near, saith the LORD; and I will heal him. But the wicked are like the troubled sea, when it cannot rest, whose waters cast up mire and dirt. There is no peace, saith my God, to the wicked."

(Isaiah 57:19-21)

The message of Isaiah is akin to that of Jude. God offers peace to repentant sinners. But for the wicked who, being like the turbulent sea, reject the longsuffering of God and from the raging and turmoil of their divided heart bring forth "mire and dirt" – those things that pollute and defile – there is but one end: "There is no peace, saith my God, to the wicked."

196

Jude expresses it differently. He describes them as "foaming out their own shame". The word rendered "shame" is plural as if to emphasise the manifold nature of their sins. Their works being as mire and dirt brought upon them nothing but shame. There was but one end for such men and Jude emphasises their destiny in the last of his five metaphors.

"Wandering stars"

Again there is an element of doubt as to the precise allusion. Some think the reference is to the comet which pursues its course across the night sky until finally lost in the darkness. But the comet does have a course; it pursues a chosen path in the heavens, so precise that men can accurately forecast its appearance.

More likely is the suggestion that the allusion is to the 'shooting star' or meteor which flashes momentarily across the night sky. We can understand how its appearance would cause consternation and even fear in the hearts of the superstitious minds of that pagan world, as it was lost in the darkness that so soon enveloped it.

But there is another possibility that we feel has a certain appeal. Is Jude in referring to a "wandering star" asking us to consider the consequences if a star or planet was to leave its appointed station and wander aimlessly across the heavens? What utter confusion would be caused to the ordered form of creation. It would provide a vivid parallel with the false teachers who brought a state of disorder and bewilderment into the lives of those who were influenced by them. Such a star would drift away into the darkness that would eventually claim it. So these apostates had no future, for there was reserved for them "the blackness of darkness for ever".

Eternal oblivion was to be their lot and to this the scriptures bear abundant testimony.

36

THE WOMAN TAKEN IN ADULTERY

JOHN'S record of the woman taken in adultery has been the subject of much debate amongst textual scholars. The RV, which rested heavily upon the fact that the section from 7:53 to 8:11 is omitted by both the Sinaitic and Vatican manuscripts, includes the verses in parenthesis. The New English Bible omits them and relegates them to the end of the Gospel as a kind of footnote. Similarly, almost all modern translators treat the passage as being of doubtful authenticity in this place in John's record, yet most still regard it as a genuine account of an event in the ministry of the Lord Jesus that has been inserted at this point for some reason. The evidence on which the textual scholars depend is, however, by no means as overwhelming as some would suggest, and while we lack the space and expertise to analyse this evidence adequately, we would refer readers to the summary included in John Carter's book, *The Gospel of John* (2006 edition, pages 104,105).

For our part we believe that the context in which this passage occurs reveals it to be an integral part of the Gospel, and any attempt to remove it from this position destroys the structure and diminishes the force of the message contained in these chapters (7 and 8) of John's Gospel.

At the Feast of Tabernacles
Chapter 7 records how the Lord Jesus came to Jerusalem and in the midst of the Feast of Tabernacles went into the temple and taught (verse 14). This would appear to be the first occasion that the Lord Jesus had openly taught in the temple. Scathingly the Jews asked,

"How knoweth this man (literally, 'fellow') letters, having never learned?" (verse 15). He had never attended the rabbinical schools; his manner of teaching was different from that of the learned in Israel, yet he spoke with an authority and understanding that impressed all who heard him. The response of the Lord Jesus was to direct them to his divine origin, emphasising that the things he taught came directly from God (verses 16-18).

Consequently there arose a dispute as to the origin of the Lord Jesus. The Jews believed that when Messiah came his parentage would be unknown, but they had investigated the circumstances of the Lord's birth thoroughly:

"Howbeit we know this man whence he is: but when Christ cometh, no man knoweth whence he is."
(verse 27)

With a loud voice the Lord Jesus cried in the temple acknowledging that from a human perspective their assessment was right. Nevertheless they had no understanding of the true nature of his origin, and again he emphasises that both he and the message he brought were from God his Father. Incensed by these words, they would have taken him by force and later sent officers to bring him into custody, all to no avail (verses 28-30,44-47).

Another point to be noted is the emphasis upon judgement. Significantly, the record of the institution of the Feast of Tabernacles in Deuteronomy is immediately followed by the command to appoint judges (Deuteronomy 16:13-20).

Almost certainly we do not have the full account of the exchanges between the Jews and the Lord Jesus, and it has been suggested that actually the debate was continued throughout the last few days of the feast and therefore some of the words were spoken on different days. The reference to the healing of the impotent man on the sabbath and the consequent illustration of circumcision taking precedence over the sabbath, together with the Lord's direct quotation of the words of Deuteronomy 16, lend credence to this possibility.

"Judge not according to the appearance, but judge righteous judgment." (John 7:24)

In their assessment of the Lord Jesus and his teaching, the Jews had failed singularly to recognise the authority by which he spoke and the wonder of the works that he performed. They were blinded by their own prejudices and the danger that they perceived was presented by the challenge of the Lord Jesus to those things they held dear.

This theme of judgement is one to which the Lord returns in Chapter 8:

"Ye judge after the flesh; I judge no man (i.e., after the flesh). And yet if I judge, my judgment is true: for I am not alone, but I and the Father that sent me."
(verses 15,16)

It is generally accepted by those who uphold the veracity of John's record that the first verse of chapter 8 belongs with the last verse of chapter 7:

"And every man went unto his own house. Jesus went unto the mount of Olives."

These simple words of fact are pregnant with significance. In fulfilment of the words of Malachi, "The LORD, whom ye seek, shall suddenly come to his temple" (3:1,2), the Lord Jesus had suddenly appeared in the temple in the midst of the feast (John 7:14). Note the emphasis on seeking in both chapters 7 and 8 of John's record (7:11,25,34-36,52; 8:21,37,40). However, they could not abide before him; they could not stand, for like a refiner's fire and fullers' soap he would have purged them of all iniquity and purified their hearts. So it was that at the end of that last day of the feast they departed every man to his own house, but the Lord Jesus went to the Mount of Olives, no doubt to the Garden of Gethsemane, that he might find strength in prayer and communion with his Father. He too had come to his own house, but those who claimed to seek the coming of the Messiah had rejected him. They had denied him his rightful place in his Father's house and, whereas they went every man to his own house, the Lord Jesus went unto the Mount of Olives.

"Taken in adultery"

It is into this context that the record of the woman taken in adultery falls (8:2-11). They brought the woman that they might tempt him, that is put him to the test, by presenting him with what they regarded as a moral dilemma. Moses had commanded that such should be stoned (Deuteronomy 22:22-24). Would he uphold the law or bring upon himself the disapproval, not only of the Council, but also of many of the ordinary people of Jerusalem for denying the words of Moses?

Alternatively, if he insisted that the penalty of the law should be carried out, then he was in danger of incurring the wrath of the Roman authority who had withdrawn from the Jews the right to inflict capital punishment except with their approval in special circumstances. He might also have caused some disillusionment among the common people, for moral standards were lax and the Galilean peasants in particular did not generally live by the standards of the law.

There was, however, something more sinister behind this approach of the scribes and Pharisees. We have already noted their interest in the origin of the Lord Jesus (John 7:27,28) and we can be certain that even if they were unaware that Joseph was not his father, they knew, from a human perspective, of the uncertainty that surrounded the circumstances of his birth. It was a matter to which they were to return on the eighth day of the feast which was celebrated as a holy convocation (Leviticus 23:36). Note the pointed question, "Where is thy Father?" (John 8:19) and the implied slanderous accusation, "*We* be not born of fornication" (verse 41).

We can only imagine what their reaction might have been if the Lord had responded to their question directly. Whatever his answer, they would have turned it to their advantage by then calling into question the events surrounding his own birth.

There is about the whole incident something that is shameful and unseemly. This woman they said was taken "in the very act" (8:4). The question has been well asked, 'Where was the man?' The fact that they brought only the woman is an indication that they had ulterior motives.

"He stooped down"

John records that the Lord Jesus "stooped down" (verse 6) and we wonder whether this action is reminiscent of Moses who, when God declared His name, "made haste, and bowed (same Greek word in the Septuagint) his head toward the earth, and worshipped" (Exodus 34:8). Remember that it was on this occasion that Moses took in his hand the two tables of stone containing the Ten Commandments (see verses 1,28) and as the Lord stood by him, heard the name of God declared:

> "The LORD, the LORD God, merciful and gracious, longsuffering, and abundant in goodness and truth, keeping mercy for thousands, forgiving iniquity and transgression and sin." (Exodus 34:6,7)

The two tablets of stone were certainly in the mind of the Lord Jesus as he stooped, but was he also thinking of that grand declaration of the mercy and lovingkindness of his Father as he looked, surely with some embarrassment, on this poor wretched woman that they had dragged so brazenly before him?

The Lord Jesus wrote on the ground with his finger, recalling the manner in which the commandments had been inscribed on the tablets by the finger of God (Exodus 31:18; Deuteronomy 9:10). What did he write? There have been many different suggestions. We believe that he began to write the Ten Commandments. "Thou shalt not commit adultery" is the seventh, but when he came to the sixth he stopped, for this was, "Thou shalt not kill" and they had come with murder in their hearts. Note that the determination of the Jews to kill him is emphasised throughout chapters 7 and 8 of John's

Gospel (7:1,19,20,25,44; 8:40,44,59). It was at this juncture as they clamoured for an answer, that the Lord Jesus declared: "He that is without sin among you, let him first cast a (literally, 'the') stone at her" (John 8:7). Perhaps James was recalling this incident when he wrote:

"For whosoever shall keep the whole law, and yet offend in one point, he is guilty of all. For he that said, Do not commit adultery, said also, Do not kill. Now if thou commit no adultery, yet if thou kill, thou art become a transgressor of the law." (2:10,11)

So the Lord Jesus, stooping again, began to write once more. What did he write now? The context of John 7 and 8 demonstrates in a most remarkable way that the account of the woman taken in adultery is an integral part of the Gospel record.

In the last great day of the feast the Lord Jesus had cried, "If any man thirst, let him come unto me, and drink" (John 7:37). Old Testament scripture brings these words and the actions of the Lord in chapter 8 together in a very significant fashion:

"O LORD, the hope of Israel, all that forsake thee shall be ashamed, and they that depart from me shall be written in the earth, because they have forsaken the LORD, the fountain of living waters."

(Jeremiah 17:13)

A comparison of the events at the Feast of Tabernacles as recorded by John with the first part of Jeremiah 17 (verses 1-18) shows a similarity of thought and insight, if not always providing precise verbal connections (see particularly verses 1,9,10,15,18).

What did the Lord write? It was surely the names of those gathered before him who had forsaken the Lord, "the fountain of living waters". Convicted by their conscience they left one by one, beginning with the eldest, until the woman was left standing alone before the Lord Jesus. They, the judges of Israel, had brought the woman before him that they might provoke him to pronounce judgement upon her. But in doing so what they accomplished was to bring judgement upon themselves.

We have already drawn attention to the emphasis upon judgement in these two chapters and it was the custom on this last day of the feast to read a portion of Psalm 82 (see Edersheim, *The Temple: its ministry and services as they were at the time of Jesus Christ*, page 285). In this psalm the judges of Israel, meeting in solemn conclave, are themselves judged because of their failure to "judge righteous judgment" and the manner in which they ignored the plight of the poor and destitute. God Himself takes the seat of the Presiding Officer:

"God standeth in the congregation of the mighty; he judgeth among the gods. How long will ye judge unjustly, and accept the persons of the wicked?"

(verses 1,2)

"Neither do I condemn thee"

When her accusers had departed, the woman stood in the throng surrounding the Lord and they no doubt were anxious to hear how he would deal with her. Some assert that she showed no faith or repentance, but the record is brief and it is hard to imagine how a woman in this situation, perhaps traumatised and bewildered by the way she had been treated, could have responded fully to these circumstances. She did, however, address Jesus as "Lord" (John 8:11) and this would appear to indicate that she had come to an understanding of the uniqueness of the one before whom she stood. Notwithstanding the manner in which the Lord had confounded her accusers, the fact remained that she had committed a grievous sin. He made no attempt to hide this fact and perhaps his command, "Go, and sin no more", was the means to assure her that if she truly repented and changed the manner of her living, she could be assured that forgiveness was freely available. It would be presumptuous of us to assume that on the basis of this incident we have the Lord's authority to treat any sin leniently, or to give assurances to any

204

individuals that their sins are forgiven, for that is the prerogative of God and the Lord Jesus alone who know the hearts and innermost thoughts of all.

We can but confidently assert that there is forgiveness with God, that He might be feared and point the way to that humble and contrite spirit that is the prerequisite of true repentance in His sight.

37

THE TRANSFIGURATION

THERE can be no doubt that at the beginning of his ministry the coming of the Lord Jesus engendered great enthusiasm and excitement among the common people (see Matthew 3:25; Mark 1:45; 3:7). However, as his ministry developed this fervour became more muted and as the last year of the Lord's life drew near it is evident that doubts and anxieties had arisen in the minds of the people:

"And Jesus went out, and his disciples, into the towns of Caesarea Philippi: and by the way he asked his disciples, saying unto them, Whom do men say that I am? And they answered, John the Baptist, but some say, Elias; and others, one of the prophets."

(Mark 8:27,28;
see also Matthew 16:13,14; Luke 9:18,19)

The change in attitude is a remarkable insight into human nature. They could believe almost anything rather than accept the truth and face up to the challenge that he posed. How encouraging for the Lord Jesus must have been the declaration of Peter and of the other apostles: "Thou art the Christ, the Son of the living God" (Matthew 16:16; Mark 8:29; Luke 9:20).

"Many of his disciples went back"

It was the miracle of the feeding of the five thousand that seems to have been the catalyst. It would appear that many among the multitude recognised this wonderful work to be a messianic act (see Psalm 132:11,15) and John records how they would have taken him by force and made him a king (John 6:14,15). However, instead of acquiescing with their desire, the Lord restrained them, refusing to allow them to behave

206

in this way and having sent the disciples to the other side of the lake, lest they should be caught up in this surge of enthusiasm, he departed into a mountain to pray.

The sense of disappointment and disillusionment that must have pervaded the multitude is not difficult for us to imagine. How much more so when, following him to the other side of the lake, the Lord delivered that remarkable discourse on the "bread of life" (John 6:26-58). In that discourse the Lord Jesus said:

"I am the living bread which came down from heaven: if any man eat of this bread, he shall live for ever: and the bread that I will give is my flesh, which I will give for the life of the world."   (verse 51)

Again he said:

"Whoso eateth my flesh, and drinketh my blood, hath eternal life; and I will raise him up at the last day. For my flesh is meat indeed, and my blood is drink indeed. He that eateth my flesh, and drinketh my blood, dwelleth in me, and I in him."

(verses 54-56)

Their perplexity is evident for they said, "This is an hard saying; who can hear it?" (verse 60) and the consequence was, "From that time many of his disciples went back, and walked no more with him" (verse 66).

It was at this juncture in his ministry that the transfiguration occurred. It was a time of crisis; the tide had turned. With the last year of his life stretching before him it was now evident to the Lord Jesus that Israel would reject him and the time that remained must be spent primarily in instructing his disciples and preparing himself for the ordeal that lay ahead. This is the setting for the transfiguration and an understanding of the background to this remarkable event helps us to appreciate its importance at this time in the ministry of the Lord Jesus.

For the remainder of our consideration we follow, primarily, Luke's record. Luke states that "there talked with him two men, which were Moses and Elias: who appeared in glory, and spake of his decease which he should accomplish at Jerusalem" (9:30,31). The fact that they appeared in glory is an indication that, however difficult it might be for us to understand, what happened was a prophecy of the kingdom. The Apostle Peter confirms this, for when writing of his experiences in "the holy mount" he says:

"For we have not followed cunningly devised fables, when we made known unto you the power and coming of our Lord Jesus Christ, but were eyewitnesses of his majesty. For he received from God the Father honour and glory, when there came such a voice to him from the excellent glory."

(2 Peter 1:16,17)

As the Lord contemplated the awful reality of the cross there was given to him this remarkable experience to strengthen him for the path that lay ahead. It was a foretaste of the kingdom; an assurance that God was faithful, and if he remained true to his mission then he could be confident of entering that "joy that was set before him" (Hebrews 11:2).

His decease

Luke's record tells us that Moses and Elias spoke to him of his decease that he should accomplish at Jerusalem. The Greek word translated "decease" is literally 'exodus' and it emphasises the fact that the Lord's life is presented to us as a 'departure'. As Israel left Egypt to meet with God so the life of the Lord Jesus was a journey, a pilgrimage that was finally to end when he was united with his Father. It is John's Gospel that emphasises this aspect of the Lord's life as on over twenty occasions phrases occur such as, "(I) depart out of this world unto the Father" (13:1) and "I go unto my Father" (14:12).

The means by which the Lord should enter into his Father's presence was indicated prophetically in the Psalms:

"For thou wilt not leave my soul in hell; neither wilt thou suffer thine Holy One to see corruption.

208

Thou wilt shew me the path of life: in thy presence is fulness of joy; at thy right hand there are pleasures for evermore." (Psalm 16:10,11)

It was to be by resurrection and ascension into heaven. But this 'exodus' could only be accomplished by first becoming "obedient unto death, even the death of the cross" (Philippians 2:8). His rejection by the people of Israel and the willing offering of his body for sin were an integral part of the 'exodus' that was to be accomplished at Jerusalem. His conversation with Moses and Elijah was concerning these things and was intended to strengthen his hand for the ordeal that lay before him.

Moses and Elijah

The question might well be asked, Why were these two characters chosen to strengthen and encourage the Lord at this time? We notice first that both these men had been privileged to have revelations of the glory of God at the same location, Horeb. Here, hidden in a cleft of the rock, Moses saw not only the "back parts" of God's physical majesty but also heard the declaration of His name:

"The LORD, The LORD God, merciful and gracious, longsuffering, and abundant in goodness and truth, keeping mercy for thousands, forgiving iniquity and transgression and sin, and that will by no means clear the guilty." (Exodus 34:6,7)

Elijah, fleeing from the wrath of Jezebel, came to this same location and hidden in what the Hebrew describes as "the cave" (surely the same cave where Moses received his revelation) the Lord passed by before him. Manifestations of a great wind, an earthquake and fire were experienced by Elijah, but in none of these was the Lord present. After these tremendous displays of physical power and might, Elijah heard a still small voice (Septuagint, "the voice of a light breath") and through this voice God spoke to him (1 Kings 19:8-15).

In the one instance there was a declaration of the character of God and in the other an indication that the supreme revelation of God was through His word, a still small voice, 'God-breathed' (2 Timothy 3:16). Thus both Moses and Elijah were privileged to see their visions consummated in the person of the Lord Jesus Christ in whom God was manifested uniquely, both in the life that he lived and in the words that he spoke. However, there was another equally compelling reason why these two men were chosen to strengthen the Lord Jesus at this time. They had both suffered rejection at the hands of God's people but had been blessed to come again in the assurance that their work had not been in vain.

In Stephen's address before the Jewish Council (Acts 7) he describes how the children of Israel rejected Moses (verses 23-29) causing him to flee to the land of Midian. "Who made thee a ruler and a judge over us?" they asked (verse 27). But a time came when Moses returned, and Stephen testified of him:

"This Moses whom they refused, saying, Who made thee a ruler and a judge? the same did God send to be a ruler and a deliverer by the hand of the angel which appeared to him in the bush." (verse 35)

First he was rejected, but the second time recognised and acknowledged.

Elijah also had known the bitterness of rejection. After his victory over the prophets of Baal he might well have thought that the hearts of the people would turn again to their God (1 Kings 18:37-39). Nevertheless their enthusiasm was short-lived and soon after he was forced to flee to Horeb. The voice that spoke with him there said, "What doest thou here, Elijah?" (19:9,13). He answered:

"I have been very jealous for the LORD God of hosts: because the children of Israel have forsaken thy covenant, thrown down thine altars, and slain thy prophets with the sword; and I, even I only, am left; and they seek my life, to take it away." (verse 14)

In his despair he thought that he alone remained true

to Israel's God, but the message of reassurance was clear:

> "Yet I have left me seven thousand in Israel, all the knees which have not bowed unto Baal, and every mouth which hath not kissed him." (verse 18)

Although it appeared to Elijah that his work had been unsuccessful, the quiet influence of God's word had still been affecting the hearts of men. It was still mighty to save and there remained seven thousand who had maintained their integrity before God.

Comfort and assurance

What words of comfort then these men could speak to the Lord Jesus as the tide turned against him and the multitudes began to desert him. They spoke of his 'exodus' that he was to accomplish at Jerusalem, and involved in the things of which they spoke was the assurance that his work was not in vain for he too would come again and be recognised as Saviour and King. This assurance was seen to be effective when first three thousand (Acts 2:41) and then five thousand (4:4) were added to the believers after the Lord's ascension into heaven.

The comfort and assurance that the Lord received from Moses and Elijah was complemented by the voice of God Himself. First, "there came a cloud, and overshadowed them" (Luke 9:34). The cloud spoke, of course, of the presence of God (see Exodus 19:9,16; 20:21, etc.). In consequence it was associated with the glory of God and, when Peter recalled their experiences in the "holy mount", he tells us that the voice that spoke to them on that occasion came from the "excellent glory" (2 Peter 1:17,18; see also 1 Kings 8:10,11).

In Matthew's Gospel the words spoken are recorded more fully than in Luke's record:

> "This is my beloved Son, in whom I am well pleased; hear ye him." (Matthew 17:5)

The final command to "hear him" is a clear reference to the prophecy of Moses in Deuteronomy 18:15:

"The LORD thy God will raise up unto thee a Prophet from the midst of thee, of thy brethren, like unto me; unto him ye shall hearken."

These words were intended primarily for the disciples, but the rest of the words spoken were directed to the Lord Jesus.

"This is my ... Son"

We note first the expression, "This is my ... Son", an undoubted reference to the words of Psalm 2:

"I will declare the decree: the LORD hath said unto me, Thou art my Son; this day have I begotten thee. Ask of me, and I shall give thee the heathen for thine inheritance, and the uttermost parts of the earth for thy possession."   (verses 7,8)

Thus the Lord was assured that he was the heir and that his Father, who was faithful, would give him the kingdom. But the Lord Jesus would have been aware also of the context in which these words occurred, for the psalm spoke of human endeavour to frustrate the purpose of God:

"Why do the heathen rage, and the people imagine a vain thing? The kings of the earth set themselves, and the rulers take counsel together, against the LORD, and against his anointed ..."   (verses 1,2)

These words were to have a fulfilment in his crucifixion (see Acts 4:23-30). But all men's efforts were futile for, "He that (sat) in the heavens (would) laugh: the Lord (would) have them in derision" (verse 4). The divine response to human pride and arrogance would be, "Yet have I set my king upon my holy hill of Zion" (verse 6). It would have been a great reassurance to the Lord Jesus to be reminded of these truths at this time of crisis in his ministry.

"In whom I am well pleased"

The second easily recognisable quotation, "in whom I am well pleased", is from Isaiah's prophecy:

> "Behold my servant, whom I uphold; mine elect, in whom my soul delighteth."   (42:1)

The immediate context spoke of his Father's ever present help. He was the one "whom I uphold" and the reference to these words on the mount of transfiguration was an acknowledgement of his victory over sin to that point in time. But Isaiah looked beyond the rejection of Israel to a still larger work:

> "I have put my spirit upon him: he shall bring forth judgment to the Gentiles … I the LORD have called thee in righteousness, and will hold thine hand, and will keep thee, and give thee for a covenant of the people, for a light of the Gentiles."   (verses 1,6)

Here was an indication of his impending death: "I will give thee for a covenant of the people", but also there were words of comfort and assurance, for "(I) will hold thine hand, and will keep thee". In this confidence the Lord Jesus could look beyond the cross to the day when he would be "for a light of the Gentiles".

"My beloved"

There is, however, the possibility of other Old Testament allusions in the declaration from heaven, for into the quotation from Psalm 2 is inserted the word "beloved". There are two passages in particular that appear to be relevant.

Firstly, when God told Abraham to offer his son Isaac for a burnt offering, He said:

> "Take now thy son, thine only son Isaac, whom thou lovest."   (Genesis 22:2,12,16)

Strong's Concordance tells us that the word rendered "only" is derived from one signifying 'unity', and by implication 'beloved'. Hence, of this son with whom there was such unity of thought and purpose, God said, 'Take now thy son, thy beloved son Isaac', and no other scripture could have spoken so poignantly to the Lord Jesus of the truth that before the crown of Psalm 2 there must come first the cross.

Secondly, there is the possibility of yet another allusion hidden in the word "beloved". In his blessing of Benjamin recorded in Deuteronomy 33, Moses said:

> "The beloved of the LORD shall dwell in safety by him; and the LORD shall cover him all the day long, and he shall dwell between his shoulders." (verse 12)

The context spoke of the care and protection that God would afford to his beloved and in this alone the Lord would have found solace. But the fact that the words were addressed to Benjamin would have given them added significance. When Benjamin was born his mother called him Benoni, the son of my sorrows, but Jacob called him Benjamin, the son of my right hand (Genesis 35:18). In this incident was reflected the truth concerning the one who would be both Son of Man and Son of God. The truths implicit in this typical incident are reflected in Psalm 80:

> "Let thy hand be upon the man of thy right hand, upon the son of man whom thou madest strong for thyself." (verse 17)

"I set my face like a flint"

The events involved in the transfiguration and particularly the words spoken from heaven had a profound effect upon the Lord Jesus at this crucial time in his ministry. Now, strengthened by this experience, with the inevitability of the cross, which of course he had always known must come, brought home to him in a most dramatic way by the changing attitude of the people, Luke records:

> "And it came to pass, when the time was come that he should be received up, he stedfastly set his face to go to Jerusalem … And they (the Samaritans) did not receive him, because his face was as though he would go to Jerusalem." (Luke 9:51,53)

Luke's record is unique in this respect for, from the transfiguration onwards, he presents the Lord Jesus as travelling to Jerusalem to accomplish "his decease". Here are some examples that illustrate the point:

214

"And he went through the cities and villages, teaching, and *journeying toward Jerusalem.*" (13:22)

"And it came to pass, as he *went to Jerusalem*, that he passed through the midst of Samaria and Galilee." (17:11)

"Then he took unto him the twelve, and said unto them, Behold, we go *up to Jerusalem ...*" (18:31)

"And when he had thus spoken, he went before, ascending *up to Jerusalem.*" (19:28)

The information is not geographical for sometimes, as in chapter 17, he is travelling north towards Galilee, but always it is a journey that will bring him eventually to Jerusalem where finally he would become obedient even unto the death of the cross. The spirit of the Lord was reflected in the words of the prophet Isaiah:

"For the Lord GOD will help me; therefore shall I not be confounded: therefore have I set my face like a flint, and I know that I shall not be ashamed." (50:7)

Psalm 145

There are a number of psalms that appear to foreshadow the Lord's transfiguration. We look particularly at Psalm 145 (but see also Psalms 42 and 43) and note how the conversation between the Lord Jesus and Moses and Elijah is reflected:

"One generation shall praise thy works to another, and shall declare thy mighty acts ... They shall speak of the glory of thy kingdom, and talk of thy power." (verses 4,11)

Note the reference to "power" in this verse. Only Mark's record tells us that the Lord Jesus used this word when he introduced the impending experience that they were to have in the mount:

"Verily I say unto you, That there be some of them that stand here, which shall not taste of death, till they have seen the kingdom of God come with power." (Mark 9:1)

If, as suggested, it is possible to detect Peter's influence in this Gospel, it is significant that he too uses the word

215

when he speaks of his experience in the "holy mount" (2 Peter 1:16-18).

Psalm 145, however, contains undoubted references to the experiences of both Moses and Elijah:

> "I will declare thy greatness. They shall abundantly utter the memory of thy great goodness, and shall sing of thy righteousness. The LORD is gracious, and full of compassion; slow to anger, and of great mercy." (verses 6-8)

The words remind us unmistakeably of Moses' experience at Horeb when the name of God was proclaimed as His glory passed by before him.

But there are verses also that remind us of the experiences of Elijah fed by the ravens, and sustained by the widow of Zarephath, raised up by the Lord when Elijah wished to die because of the sense of isolation that he felt:

> "The LORD upholdeth all that fall, and raiseth up all those that be bowed down. The eyes of all wait upon thee; and thou givest them their meat in due season. Thou openest thine hand, and satisfiest the desire of every living thing." (verses 14-16)

Conclusion

Our considerations have covered the change in the attitude of the people towards the Lord Jesus as his ministry progressed, demonstrating that it was the feeding of the five thousand that proved the catalyst in this development. At this time of crisis in his ministry it was important that the Lord be strengthened to travel the way of the cross that now lay before him. It was the transfiguration that fulfilled this purpose in reminding him of the joy that was set before him through the experiences of faithful men of past ages and the fidelity of his Heavenly Father. It was the encouragement that the Lord Jesus received from this event that enabled him with such fortitude to set his face steadfastly to go up to Jerusalem.

38

OBADIAH

IN preparing a recent study, we referred to several commentaries on the prophecy of Obadiah, of which *The Twelve Minor Prophets* by George Adam Smith is a typical example. Although the book is the shortest in the Old Testament, many writers regard it as fraught with difficulty and believe it to be the work of more than one writer. The primary reason for this attitude is their unwillingness to accept the predictive element of the book (in particular verses 10-26), which they assert describes so accurately the conduct of Edom at the siege and capture of Jerusalem by Nebuchadnezzar in 586 BC that it could only have been written after the event.

This view is summed up by Smith when he writes: "The suggestion has been made, and it is plausible, that Obadiah speaks as an eye-witness of that awful time. Certainly there is nothing in the rest of the prophecy … to lead us to bring it further down than the years following the destruction of Jerusalem. Everything points to the Jews still being in exile."

(Volume 2, page 171)

It is a strange thing that a number of those who maintain that the latter part of the prophecy is post-exilic are quite happy to regard the first part as being of a much earlier date. It is noteworthy that there is no reference to Assyria or Babylon in the book. To say the least this is odd if the book was written after the exile.

Structure of the Book

The book can be divided into four clearly identified sections, the first three describing God's anger and judgements against Edom and the final section telling of Israel's ultimate blessing and exaltation.

217

1. *Introduction* (verses 1,2): God speaks of the things that follow as if they were already completed, to emphasise the immutability of His word and the fact that nothing can frustrate His will.

2. *Judgements that are to fall upon Edom* (verses 3-9): those nations Edom had previously regarded as her friends and associates were now to bring judgements on her. They are to treat her as she had previously treated Israel. Note in this section the close similarity of language between Obadiah and Jeremiah 49:7-16. It is generally accepted that because of the construction of the Hebrew text and the lack of words typical of Jeremiah's prophecy, that it is Jeremiah who is quoting Obadiah and this of course leads to the confusion in the thinking of critics as to the probability (in their minds) that Obadiah's prophecy is the work of more than one writer.

3. *Esau's hatred of Israel* (verses 10-16): this is described and the manner in which they had taken advantage of Israel's calamity to add to the suffering of God's people. Note that they are rarely the main aggressors but rather behave like scavengers – opportunists who like ravenous birds of prey seek to feed on the carcase of a dead animal. It should be noted in this section that the tenses of the verbs in verses 13 and 14 could be past or future, and this indefiniteness is a feature to which we shall refer later.

4. God will fulfil His promise to Israel (verses 17-21): Israel will ultimately be blessed and they will possess the lands promised to them when "the kingdom shall be the LORD's". In this section the verbs are all in the future tense, directing our attention to a time yet to come.

The Message

Much of the difficulty surrounding the book arises from the fact that it carries no indication as to the time when it was written and, other than his name, no means of identifying the author.

Interestingly, discounting the capture of Jerusalem by Shishak in the days of Rehoboam, there are four recorded occasions when Jerusalem was captured by invading armies:

1. The attack by the Philistines and the Arabians in the reign of Jehoram.
2. Nebuchadnezzar's first invasion when Jehoiakim was on the throne.
3. The second Chaldean assault when Jehoiachin was taken prisoner.
4. The final assault in the days of Zedekiah when the people were carried into captivity in Babylon.

On any one, if not all of these occasions the Edomites could have behaved in the manner described by the prophet.

There was also the occasion in the reign of King Jehoshaphat when the Edomites were confederate with the Moabites and the Ammonites (2 Chronicles 20:10,11) and, after making earnest prayer to God, Judah was delivered when the Moabites and the Ammonites turned against the inhabitants of Seir (verses 22-25). We mention this last instance because some have conjectured that the author of the prophecy was the Obadiah of the royal princes whom Jehoshaphat sent to teach in the cities of Judah (2 Chronicles 17:7).

Having considered the author and historical setting of the book, the question now that needs to be asked, however, is this: If these facts were important for us to know would not God have told us? That they are omitted is surely an indication that they are not necessary to an understanding of the message of the prophecy.

The fact that the verbs in verses 13 and 14 can be either past or future is particularly significant. The indefiniteness is an indication that the prophecy is, in a sense, timeless.

The subject of the book is the perpetual antagonism of the Edomites towards the people of Israel – a bitterness and hatred that began with Jacob and Esau and continued down through the centuries in the history of the two peoples. In this sense the prophecy has a recurring fulfilment and describes the animosity of Edom towards Israel whenever the opportunity presented itself. Ezekiel describes it as the "perpetual hatred" (35:5), and other instances of the cruelty and hostility of Edom towards Israel can be found scattered throughout the prophetic writings (see, for example, Psalm 137; Ezekiel 25:12-14; Joel 3:19; Amos 1:11,12).

Final reflections

In his condemnation of Edom, Obadiah likens them to the nations generally:

"For the day of the LORD is near upon all the heathen; as thou hast done, it shall be done unto thee: thy reward shall return upon thine own head. For as ye have drunk upon my holy mountain, so shall all the heathen drink continually, yea, they shall drink, and they shall swallow down, and they shall be as though they had not been."

(verses 15,16)

The Edomites, because of their origin and close association with Israel, had occupied a privileged position (see Deuteronomy 2:4-8; 23:7,8). They had, however, behaved like the nations generally and because of this they become a type of them. They followed in the footsteps of Esau who was an idolater, a fornicator and a profane person who sold his birthright for a morsel of meat (Hebrews 12:15-17). He was a worldly-minded man; the Edomites followed his example and they come to stand for the world generally (see Isaiah 34:1-10).

So indeed:

220

"The house of Jacob shall possess their possessions. And the house of Jacob shall be a fire, and the house of Joseph a flame, and the house of Esau for stubble, and they shall kindle in them, and devour them; and there shall not be any remaining of the house of Esau; for the LORD hath spoken it."

(verses 17,18)

SCRIPTURE REFERENCE INDEX

226

228

229